ONDORI

# POP-UP
## Best Greeting Cards

ORIGAMIC ARCHITECTURE
BY
KEIKO NAKAZAWA

ONDORI

# CONTENTS

## Pop-Up BEST GREETING CARDS

FUNDAMENTALS OF ORIGAMIC ARCHITECTURE

**Author: Keiko Nakazawa**
**Born in Nagoya, Japan**
**Graduated Shukutoku High School**
**Licensed Japanese Dance Teacher**
**Opened Private School**
**1983: Studied Origamic Architecture**

★Copyright ⓒ 1995 KEIKO NAKAZAWA & ONDORISHA PUBLISHERS., LTD. All rights reserved.
★Published by ONDORISHA PUBLISHERS., LTD.,
　11-11 Nishigoken-cho, shinjuku-ku, Tokyo 162, Japan.
★Sole Overseas Distributor:Japan Publications Trading CO Ltd.
　P. O. Box 5030 Tokyo International, Tokyo, Japan.
★Distributed
・in United States by Kodansha America, INC.
　114 Fifth Avenue, New York, NY 10011, U. S. A.
・in Canada by Fitzhenry & Writeside LTD.
　195 Allstate Parkway, Markham, Ontario L3R 4T8, Canada.
・in British Isles & European Continent by Premier Book Marketing Ltd.,
　1 Gower Street, London WCIE 6HA, England.
・in Australia by Bookwise International.
　54 Crittenden Road, Findon, South Australia 5023, Australia.
・in The Far East and Japan by Japan Publications Trading Co, Ltd.,
　1-2-1, Sarugaku-cho, Chiyoda-ku, Tokyo 101, Japan

10　9　8　7　6　5　4　3　2　1

ISBN 0-87040-964-6
Printed in Japan

① pattern on page 48  ② pattern on page 60

❶

❷

# ◆FLOWER TALE

❸

③ pattern on page 51
④ pattern on page 55

# ◆NATURE SCENE

❺

❻

Front

Back

# ◇ GIFT CARD

⑪

⑫

⑬

⑭

11

# ◇GREETING CARD (90°)

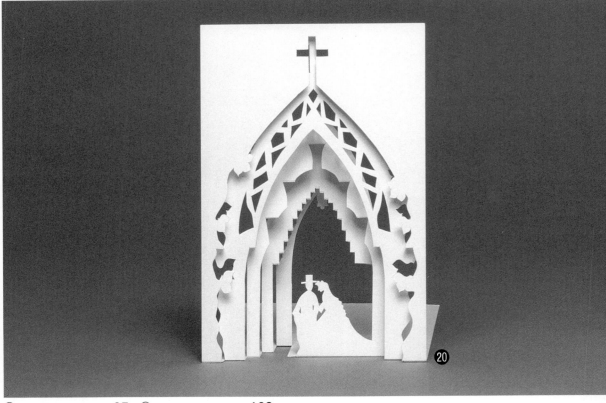

㉑ pattern on page 27　㉒ pattern on page 108
㉑ pattern on page 110

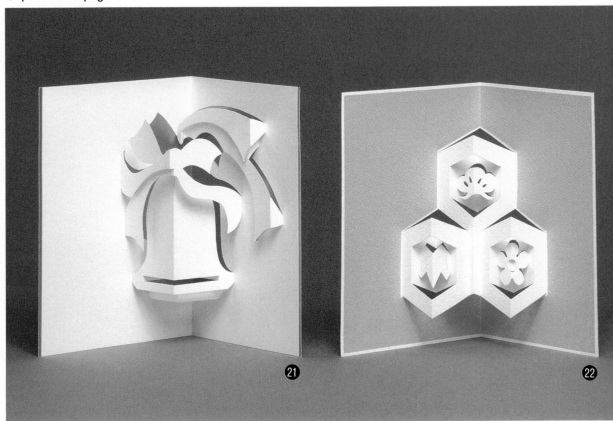

㉓ pattern on page 112   ㉕ pattern on page 109
㉔ pattern on page 111

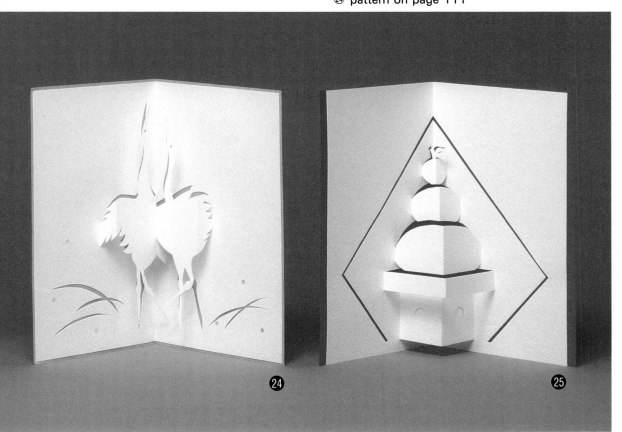

# ◆ GREETING CARD (180°)

㉖ pattern on page 89
㉗ pattern on page 92

㉖

㉗

14

㉘

㉙

㉚

31 pattern on page 29
32 pattern on page 35
33 pattern on page 38
34 pattern on page 42

# ◇CELEBRATIONS

# ◇BOUQUET

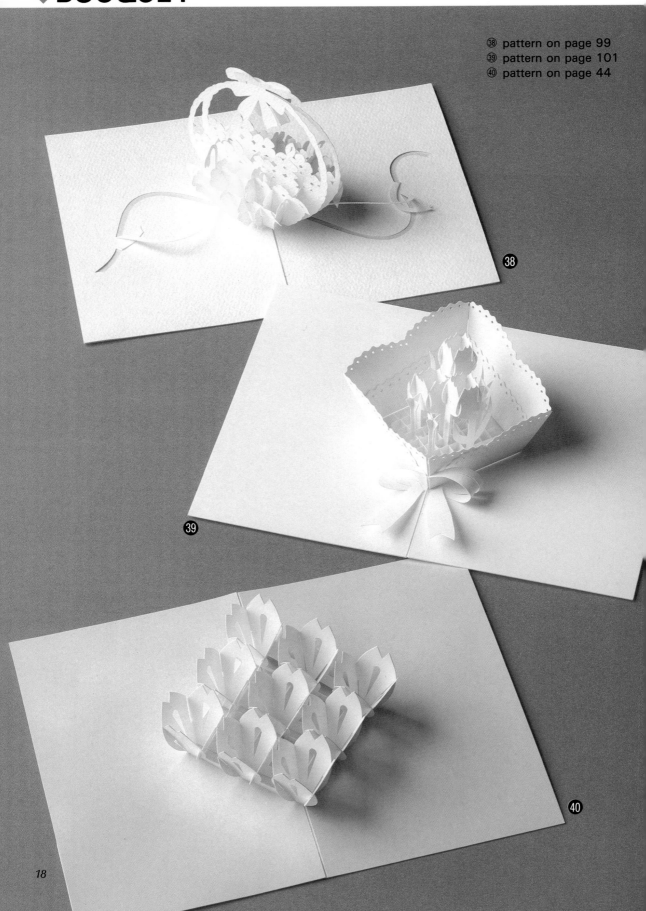

㊳

㊴

㊵

④ pattern on page 44   ④ and ④ pattern on page 118

# ◇ALPHABET CARD

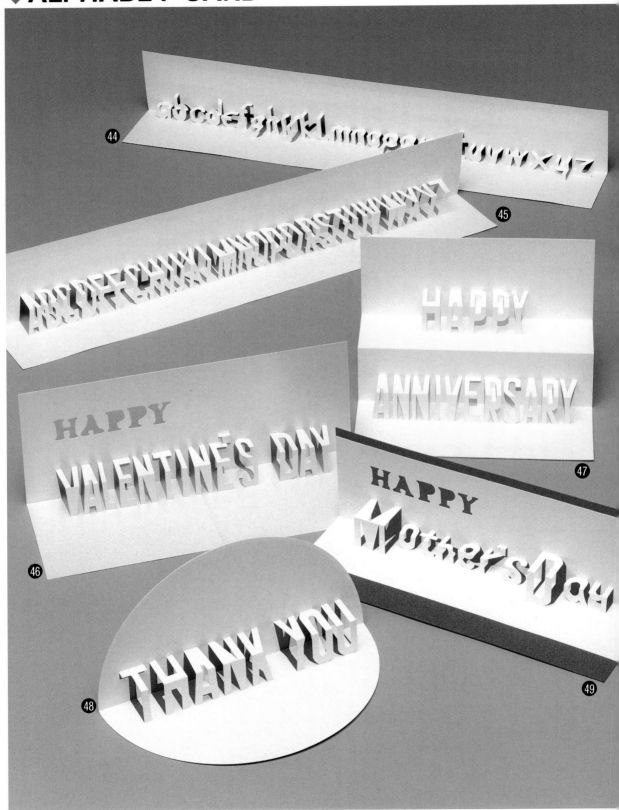

44 pattern on page 121  47 pattern on page 106
45 pattern on page 120  48 pattern on page 104
46 pattern on page 105  49 pattern on page 107

# BASICS IN ORIGAMIC ARCHITECTURE

## Materials and Tools

● All the designs shown in this book can be made using simple materials and tools, but your hands and head are the mostimportant tools. Do your best to improve on the crafts by using not only white paper, but also various colored papers.

You should personalize the crafts by using your favorite colors, not just those in the examples. This time we do not pay attention to size to make the unique 0° craft called "Silhouette" which is larger than typical European greeting cards.

● **Basic Materials and Tools**

[Materials]
・White Bristol paper, colored Bristol paper
・White duna paper, colored duna paper (use a thick paper with a rough surface)
・Metallic paper (reflecting surface)
・Japanese rice paper (thin, strong paper to strengthen the craft and for gluing parts)
・Tracing paper
・White cotton thread (to attach craft to the base)
・All purpose glue (fast drying glue for paper)
・Drafting tape (for temporary attachment of craft and thread to the Bristol paper)

[Tools]
・Cutting mat
・Cutting knife (a circle cutter or design cutter work well for cutting curves)
・Steel ruler
・Stylus (fine tip for making holes and wide tip for tracing lines)
・Tweezers (with a sharp tip for making fine folds in 90° crafts, attaching Japanese rice paper to the 180°crafts, and attaching thread to the base)

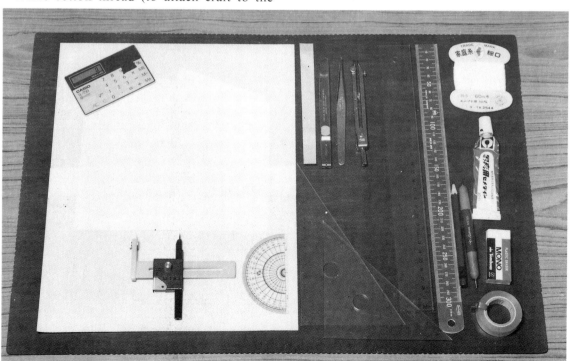

# PRACTICE IN MAKING ORIGAMIC ARCHITECTURE

## 1) Pointers for Making Origamic Architecture

### ① How to cut the pattern

Place the traced pattern on a sheet of Bristol paper and transfer the pattern by perforating with a stylus. Using the cutting knife and steel ruler, cut along the perforated lines. When cutting sharp angles, cut each side toward the point. For curves, use circle cutter or draw curves with a pencil and cut along pencil lines freehand. Curves are best cut by moving both the paper and the cutter. These crafts involve much more joining of pieces than in previous editions, so it is important that the pattern be followed closely at irregular points and in making the lengths and widths of grooves. If the depth of the groove is wrong, the sides will not fit together correctly. Another key point is to begin cutting pieces by cutting the narrowest grooves. After cutting all the grooves, cut the outline. Make sure the cutting is done exactly along the lines.

### HOW TO CUT SHARP ANGLES

### ② How to crease

A stylus is usually used for creasing. For a valley fold line score on the front side and for a mountain fold line score on the back. To make neat fold lines, cut to a depth of one-third of the paper on the front side. To make creation of your design easier and the final product more beautiful and work well, cut one-third way through the paper before making mountain or valley folds. Another way to do this is to put only the lightest pressure on the cutter and trace the pattern. In this way, mountain folds are cut on the front side and valley folds are cut on the back side.

### ③ How to glue the paper

Use all-purpose glue for assembling. It is not necessary to cover the entire surface. Be careful when putting glue near edges.

### ④ How to fold in half

In crafts which have a base, both papers must be folded so no edges protrude. If care is taken when crafts are being made, the edges should not protrude. If edges do protrude, place a steel ruler along the protruding edges and cut them off.

## PROPER HANDLING OF PAPER

Fold lines should be put at right angles to grain of the paper. Both Bristol paper and duna paper are used in making origamic architecture in this book. The finished designs will look neat when they are handled properly. In the paper-making process, wood fibers tend to line up lengthwise, so most papers have a grain. When the wood fibers are aligned parallel to the long side of the paper it is called lengthwise-grain paper, and when the fibers are aligned parallel to the short side of the paper it is called crosswise-grain paper. When making 90-degree open-type designs, use lengthwise-grain paper. Paper is strongest when folded against the grain; when paper is folded with the grain it tends to bend and curl. To determine the grain of your paper, bend a 10cm (4") square. If the paper is easily folded, it has a lengthwise grain, if not, it has a crosswise grain.

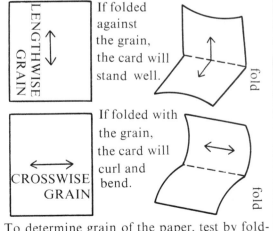

If folded against the grain, the card will stand well.

If folded with the grain, the card will curl and bend.

To determine grain of the paper, test by folding.

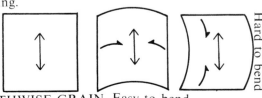

LENGTHWISE GRAIN  Easy to bend

## 2) How to Make Original Crafts (Application)

### ① Sketch

Decide which pop up design you can make by studying landscape photos and art in books and magazines. If you think you canmake the design, make a sketch of it and develop a characteristic motif.

### ② Making your pattern

Transfer your sketch to graph paper. To ensure that the finished design fits on the paper, be sure to make a fold line across themiddle of the sheet and check that the pattern does not extend past the edges of the sheet.

### ③ Prototype

After finishing the pattern, make the design using any craft at hand.

### ④ Improvement

As you make your prototype, you will discover the best places for cutting and folding, as well as places where these should beavoided.

### ⑤ Full size pattern

After noting the improvements, draw the full size pattern, keeping in mind as you work the order of cutting and folding.

### ⑥ Completing the design

Trace the final pattern onto tracing paper. Place a sheet of Bristol paper beneath the tracing paper and perforate at the cornerswith a stylus. Connect the perforated points following the lines of the pattern. Proceed with cutting and folding of the lines. Follow the instructions of this book in making mountain and valley folds and you will have made your very own origamiarchitecture!

### ⑦ Adding accents

Study the whole design to see where you can best use colored papers for effective accents.

# STEP-BY-STEP INSTRUCTIONS FOR MAKING DESIGNS (1)

## 0° Craft (⑨JAPANESE PAGODA)

① Materials          **Shown on page 9**

1 Sheet white duna paper 15cm × 20cm (6″ × 8″)
1 Sheet color duna paper 15cm × 20cm (6″ × 8″)

② Attach the copy onto each duna paper with drafting tape. Follow by copying the curved lines with the stylus.

③ Remove the pattern and carefully cut the pieces following the pattern.

④ Score on the back of the paper, since the center of the two sheets is a valley fold.

⑤ Refer to the diagram to assemble the parts cut from the two sheets of paper.

⑥ Glue together with the backs of the assembled pieces on the bottom and the front on top.

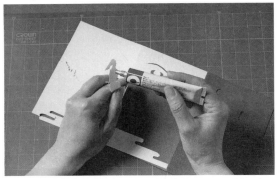

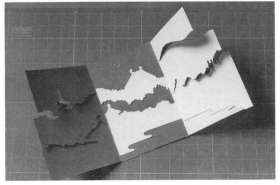

⑦ Fold together from the top as shown in the photo (valley fold).

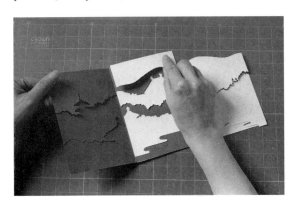

⑧ Close by inserting into slot.

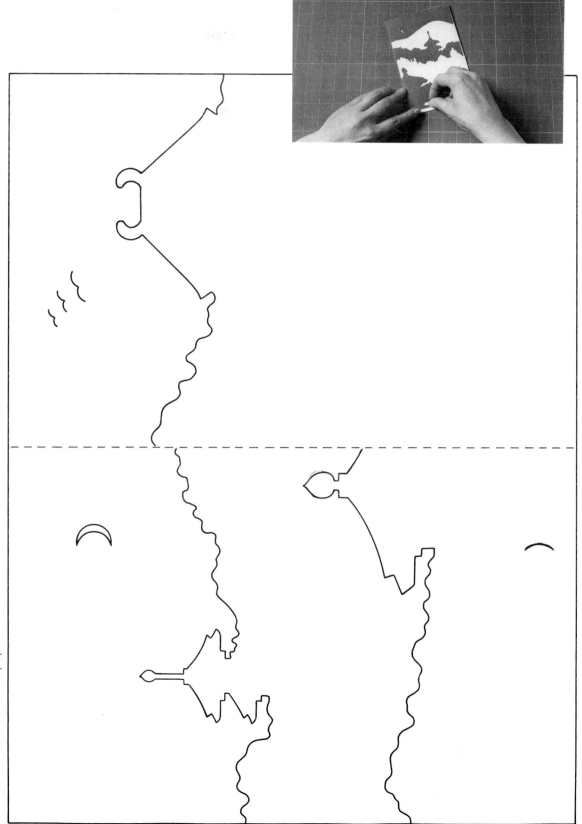

Dark colored duna paper

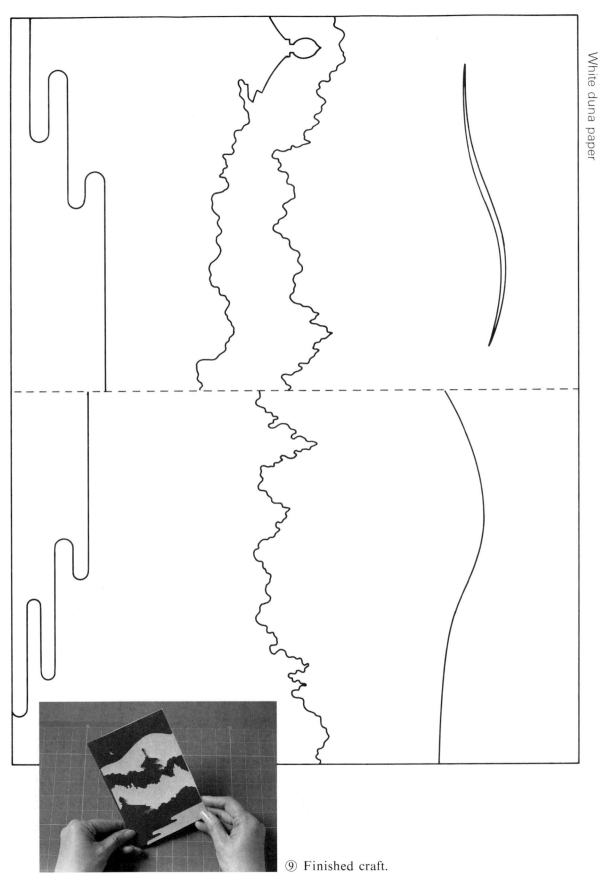

White duna paper

⑨ Finished craft.

Front                              Back

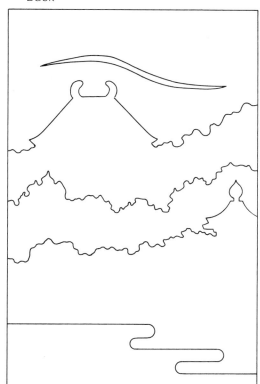

# STEP-BY-STEP INSTRUCTIONS FOR MAKING DESIGNS (2)

## 90° Craft (⑳ White Chapel)

**Shown on page 12**

① Materials: 1 sheet white Bristol paper, 10cm × 30cm (4″ × 12″)

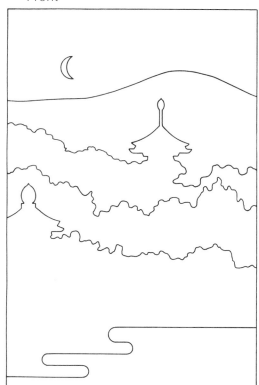

② Attach the copy to the sheet of Bristol paper and copy by tracing with a stylus. Using the stylus, perforate along the dottedline. Copy the curved line.

③ Compare the traced pattern with the original to check for errors.

④ Cut along cutting line, using the ruler to cut the straight lines.

27

⑤ Score along fold lines on the back for mountain folds and on the front for valley folds.

⑥ Using tweezers, slowly fold mountain and valley folds as shown in the diagram. Pay attention to the movement of your lefthand.

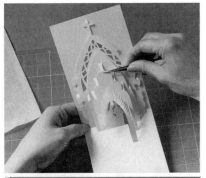

⑦ Fold tight and straighten out the shape.

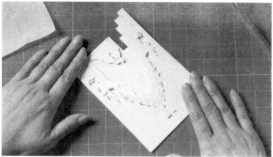

⑧ Gradually fold open.

⑨ Finished craft.

# STEP-BY-STEP INSTRUCTIONS FOR MAKING DESIGNS (3)

## 180° CRAFT (㉛ JAPANESE DOLL AND ㉜ ENVELOPE)

**Shown on page 16**

① Materials

4 Sheets white duna paper 15cm × 20cm (6″ × 8″)

1 Sheet gold paper 15cm × 20cm (6″ × 8″)

1 Strip patterned paper 1.5cm × 15cm (½″ × 6″)

Japanese rice paper and 3 pieces of thread about 15cm (6″)

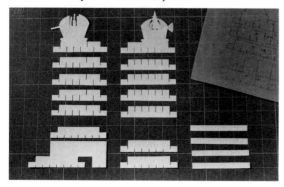

② Copy the pattern onto duna paper in order and carefully cut out the parts.

③ Fold the emperor and empress as shown in the diagram.

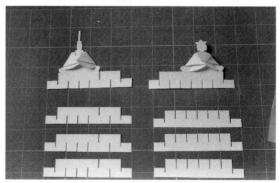

④ Assemble parts in order.

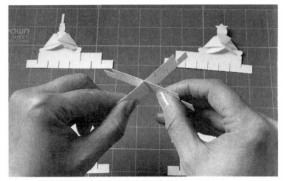

⑤ Connect border with Japanese rice paper.

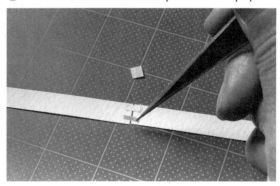

⑥ Attach border to completed platform. It is not necessary to connect the border all around. Connecting at two or three pointson each side should make it strong enough.

⑦ Refer to the assembly pattern and attach threads at the proper locations.

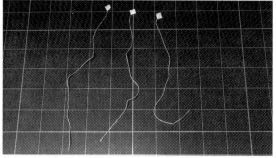

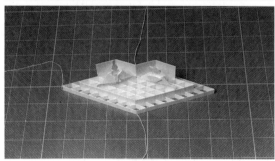

⑧ Make the base. Attach 15cm × 15cm (6″ × 6″) and 15cm × 9cm (6″ × 3½″) base paper using a 1cm × 15cm (½ × 6″) strip of Japanese rice paper, leaving a 1mm (1/16″) gap between the sheets.

⑨ Glue the gold colored paper to the back of the white paper. Glue the gold colored paper to the 9cm (3½″) base sheet leaving 2mm (1/16″) extending from the edge. Glue the patterned paper to the back of this. (The patterned paper should extend 8mm(¼″) from the edge.)

⑩ Perforate the base paper as shown on the diagram. Insert the thread through the hole using the tweezers.

⑪ Lightly attach thread at three places with drafting tape.

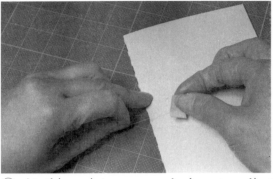

⑫ At this point, open and close to adjust movement of thread.

⑬ After adjusting thread movement, attach thread with glue as closely as possible to the hole using Japanese rice paper. Trimextra thread and remove drafting tape.

⑭ Attach reinforcement paper with glue.

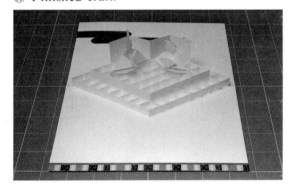

⑮ Finished craft.

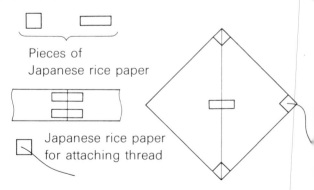

These crafts (JAPANESE DOLL AND 3-D DIE) have pieces that must be joined. They must be connected firmly to open andclose smoothly. If they do not open and close properly, the craft may break. Even though it may seem troublesome, please takethe time to join the parts with small pieces of Japanese rice paper. Also, as in other crafts, use small pieces of Japanese ricepaper whenever you feel it is necessary to strengthen the work.

Pieces of
Japanese rice paper

Japanese rice paper
for attaching thread

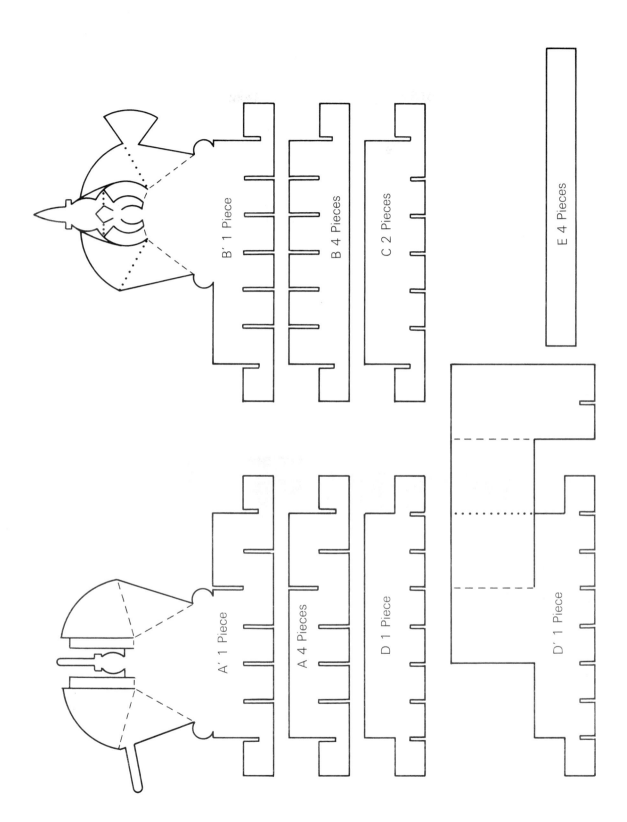

B' 1 Piece

B 4 Pieces

C 2 Pieces

E 4 Pieces

A' 1 Piece

A 4 Pieces

D 1 Piece

D' 1 Piece

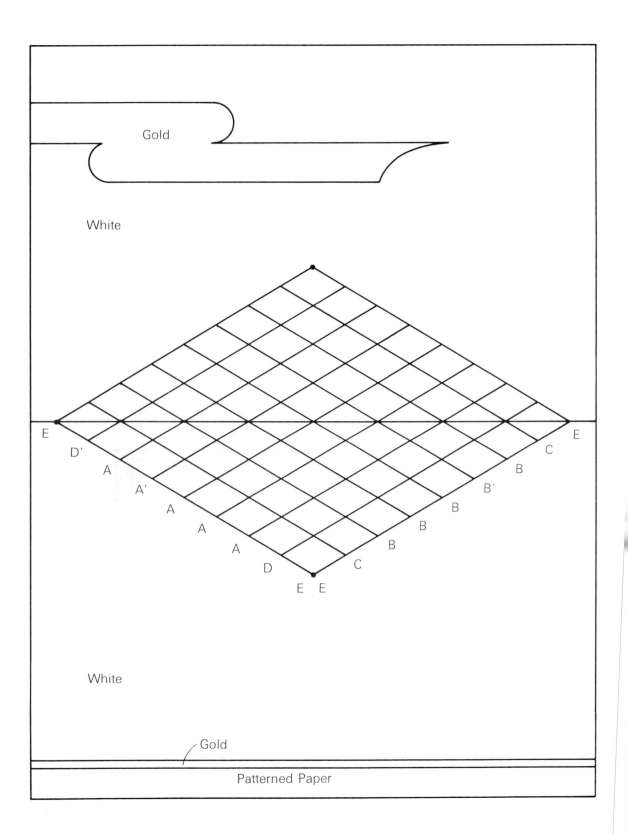

# ENVELOPE

① Materials:

1 Sheet gold paper 16.5cm × 36cm (6½″ × 14¼″)
1 Sheet red duna paper 15cm × 20cm (6″ × 8″)

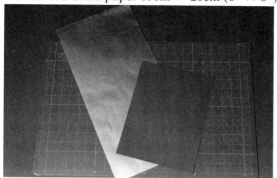

② Lay the pattern on the gold colored paper and make grooves for folds with the stylus.

③ Lay the parts diagram on the red duna paper and make marks with the stylus. Cut out pieces.

④ Score the back of the paper with the cutter knife. (The paper is very thin, so simply trace the pattern.)

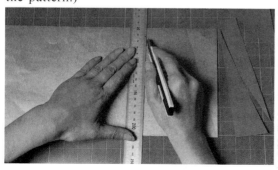

⑤ Make the mountain and valley folds in order.

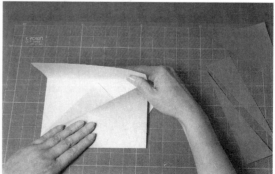

⑥ Gold colored paper with completed folds.

⑦ Glue the red duna paper to the back of the gold colored paper, leaving 2mm (116″) extending from edge A.

⑧ Glue edge B of the red duna paper to the un-folded part of the gold paper.

⑨ Insert the remaining red duna paper C into the folded part of the gold paper.

3.0(1¼")

6.5(2½")

10.0(4")

12.0(4¾")

11.0(4⅜")

11.5(4½")

2.0(¾")

Finished size
11.5cm × 16.5cm (4½" × 6½")
(A 16.5cm × 36cm (6½" × 14¼")
sheet is required)

16.5(6½")

11.5(4½")

16.5(6½")

6.0(2⅜")

36.0(14¼")

10.5(4¼")

4.5(1¾")

36

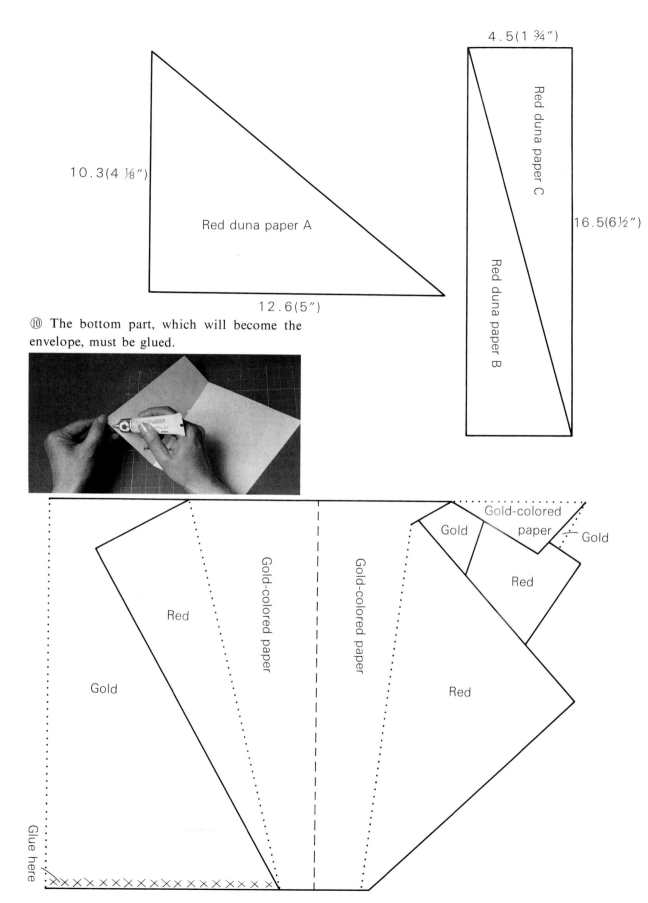

10.3(4 ⅛″)

Red duna paper A

12.6(5″)

4.5(1 ¾″)

Red duna paper C

16.5(6½″)

Red duna paper B

⑩ The bottom part, which will become the envelope, must be glued.

Red

Gold

Gold-colored paper

Gold-colored paper

Red

Gold-colored paper

Gold

Gold

Red

Red

Glue here

×××××××××××××××××××××

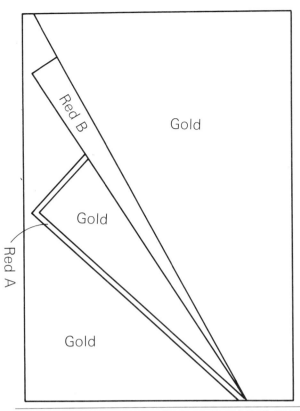

Red B

Gold

Red A

Gold

Gold

⑪ Insert the protruding edge of the gold paper into the envelope.

⑫ Finished craft.

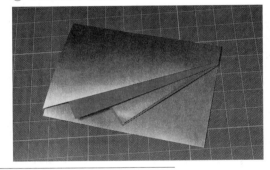

## STEP-BY-STEP INSTRUCTIONS FOR MAKING CRAFTS (4)

### NEW 180° CRAFTS (㉝ MOUNTED WARRIOR AND ㉞ ENVELOPE)

**Shown on page 16**

① Materials:
3 Sheets white Bristol paper 15cm × 20cm (6″ × 8″)
1 Sheet gold colored paper 15cm × 20cm (6″ × 8″)
1 Strip Japanese patterned paper 1.5cm × 15cm (½″ × 6″)
1 Strip Japanese rice paper 1.5cm × 15cm (½″ × 6″)

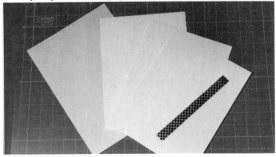

② Lay the pattern on the Bristol paper and trace with the stylus

③ Remove the pattern and cut along the cut lines, paying close attention to the pattern.

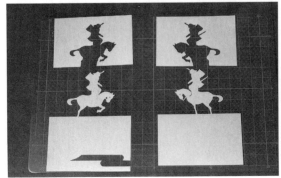

④ Using the cutter knife, score along fold lines

⑤ Fold along fold lines.

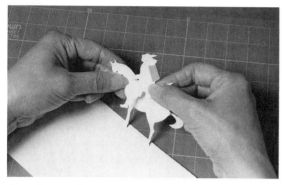

⑥ Glue craft together with a 1cm (3/8″) strip of Japanese rice paper, leaving a 1mm (1/16″) gap between.

⑦ Attach helmet, head, and back end of horse with glue.

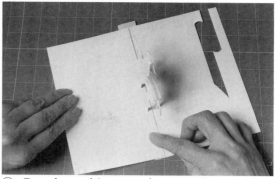

⑧ Cut the gold paper into a 15cm × 10cm (6″ × 4″) and a 15cm × 9.2cm (6″ × 3⅝″) sheet. Glue one sheet of gold to the back of the sheet with no clouds, leaving 2mm (1/16″) extended from the edge.

⑨ Cut two 15cm × 10cm (6″ × 4″) PAtterned paper of Bristol paper. Glue a strip of patterned paper to the edge, glue gold paper to the patterned paper, leaving 2mm (1/16″) extended from the edge.

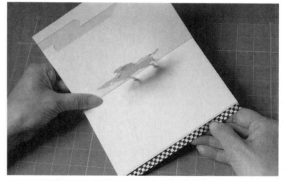

40

⑩ Finished craft.

Gold

Patterned papre

# ENVELOPE

① Prepare a 21.5cm × 31cm (8½″ × 12¼″) sheet of Japanese rice paper

② Place the pattern on the Japanese rice paper. Score at fold lines with a stylus.

③ Fold as shown. (A cutter is not necessary as it is rice paper.)

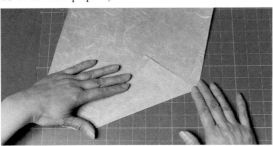

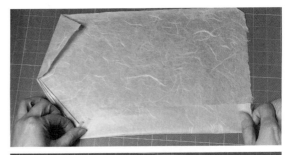

④ After folding, roll the folded back portion and it will form an envelope.

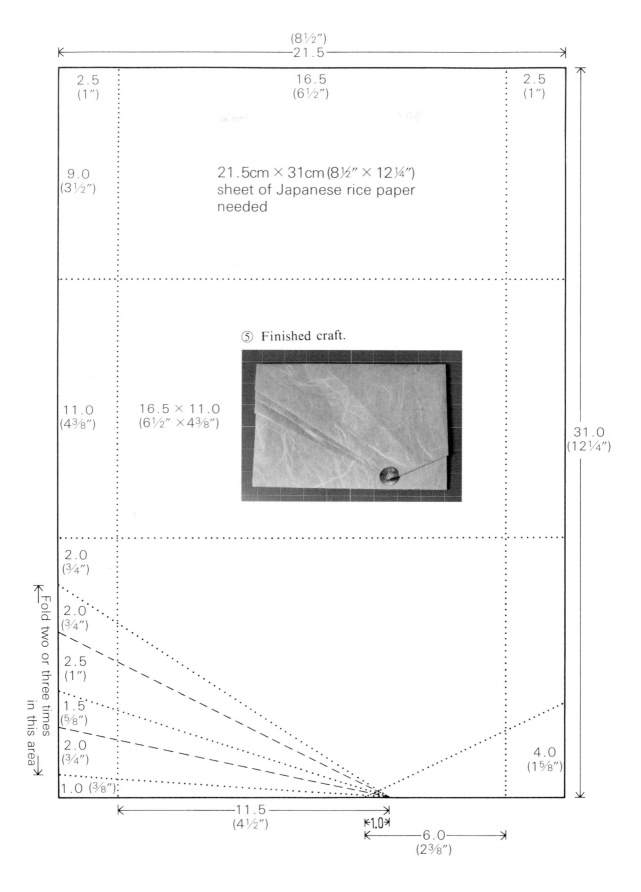

(8½")
21.5

2.5
(1")

16.5
(6½")

2.5
(1")

9.0
(3½")

21.5cm × 31cm (8½" × 12¼")
sheet of Japanese rice paper
needed

⑤ Finished craft.

11.0
(4⅜")

16.5 × 11.0
(6½" × 4⅜")

31.0
(12¼")

2.0
(¾")

2.0
(¾")

Fold two or three times
in this area

2.5
(1")

1.5
(⅝")

2.0
(¾")

4.0
(1⅝")

1.0 (⅜")

11.5
(4½")

1.0

6.0
(2⅜")

## 360° Craft (㊶ 3-D Die)

① Materials:

**Shown on page 19**

3 Sheets white Bristol paper 15cm × 20cm (6″ × 8″)

1 Sheet red glossy paper 4cm × 4cm (1⅝″ × 1⅝″)

1 Sheet black glossy paper 10cm × 20cm (4″ × 8″)

Japanese rice paper thread

② Attach pattern to the Bristol paper and score at line intersections with a stylus.

③ Punch holes in the sections you cut off. A leather punch is useful for this.

④ Cut off the triangular pieces after punching the holes.

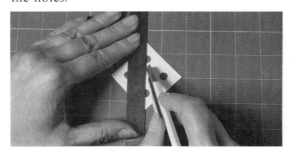

⑤ Cut out triangular pieces.

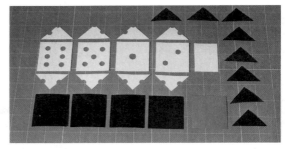

⑥ Refer to the assembly pattern and assemble using Japanese rice paper, taking care that it does not extend to the holes. (Glue at three points along each side.)

⑦ Glue along three sides.

⑧ Attach thread as shown in attachment chart.

⑨ Glue colored paper to the back. (One dot is red, the others black.)

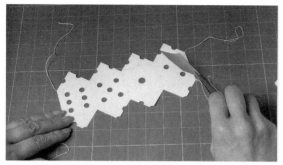

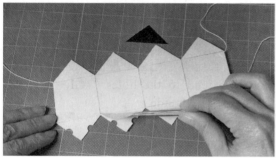

⑩ Attach reinforcement sheet to the back with small pieces of Japanese rice paper.

⑪ Glue with Japanese rice paper to create a three dimensional shape.

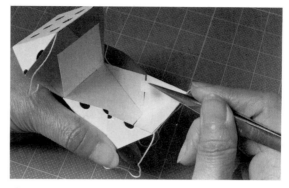

⑫ Score thread placements with a stylus and make the base.

⑬ Use Japanese rice paper to glue reinforcement to the base with the die attached.

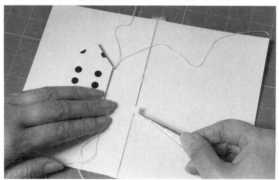

⑭ Make holes for thread placement and pass thread through with tweezers.

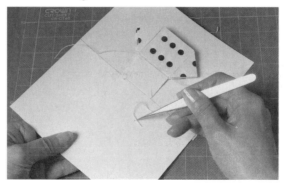

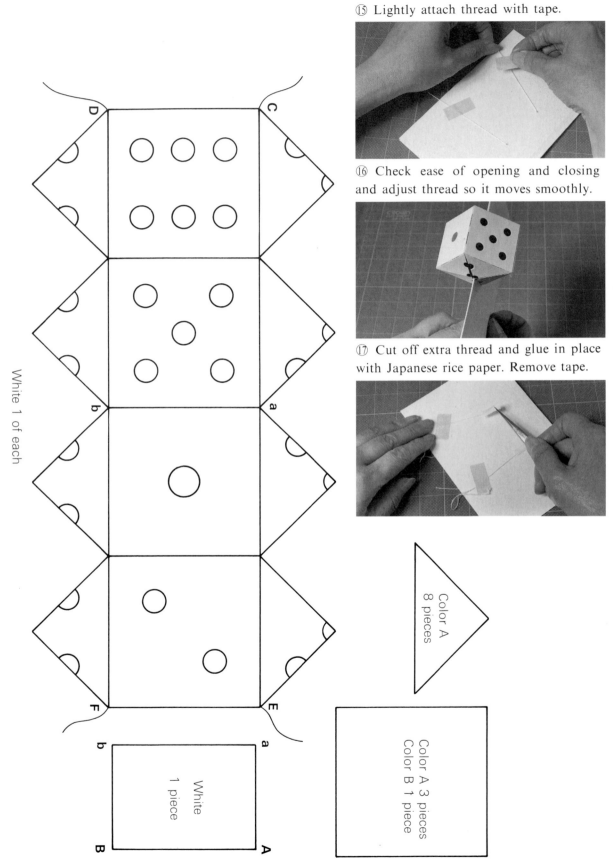

⑮ Lightly attach thread with tape.

⑯ Check ease of opening and closing and adjust thread so it moves smoothly.

⑰ Cut off extra thread and glue in place with Japanese rice paper. Remove tape.

White 1 of each

D    C

b    a

F    E

Color A
8 pieces

Color A 3 pieces
Color B 1 piece

b    a

White
1 piece

B    A

⑱ Glue reinforcement to the back.　⑲ Finished craft.

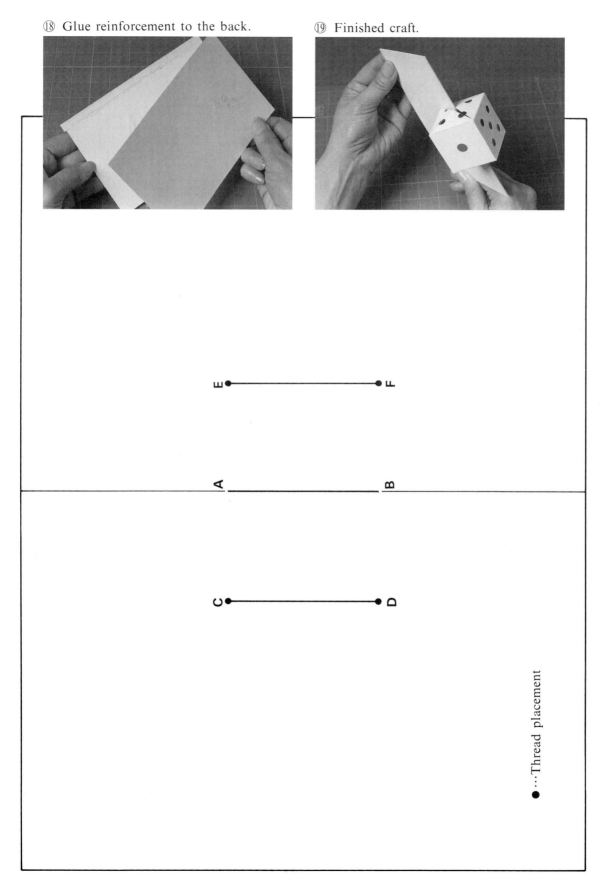

E●————————●F

A ———————————— B

C●————————●D

●⋯Thread placement

# PATTERNS AND INSTRUCTIONS

**Materials:**
2 Sheets white duna paper
30cm × 21cm (12″ × 8¼″)
1 Sheet colored duna paper
30cm × 21cm (12″ × 8¼″)
4 Sheets white duna paper
16cm × 22cm (6¼″ × 8″)
Japanese rice paper
Thread

## ① CHRISTMAS TREE
### Shown on page 5

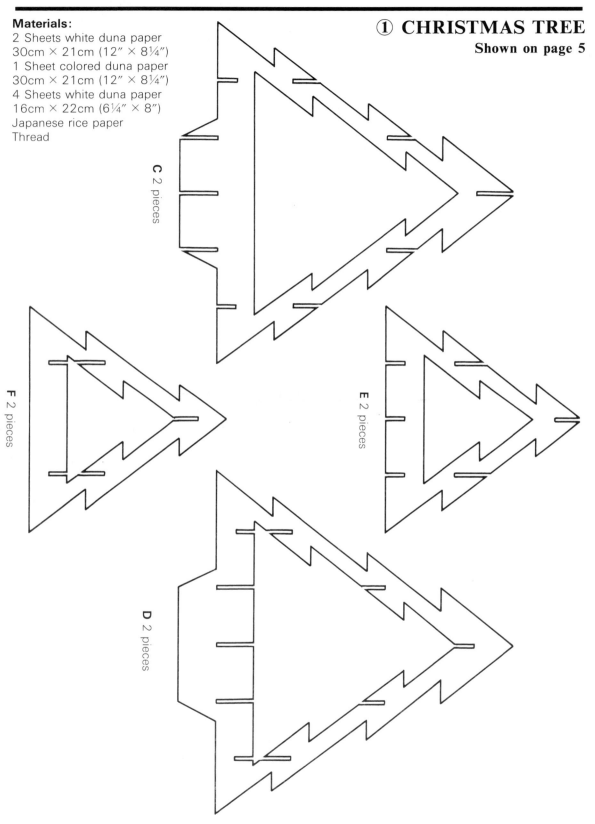

C 2 pieces

F 2 pieces

E 2 pieces

D 2 pieces

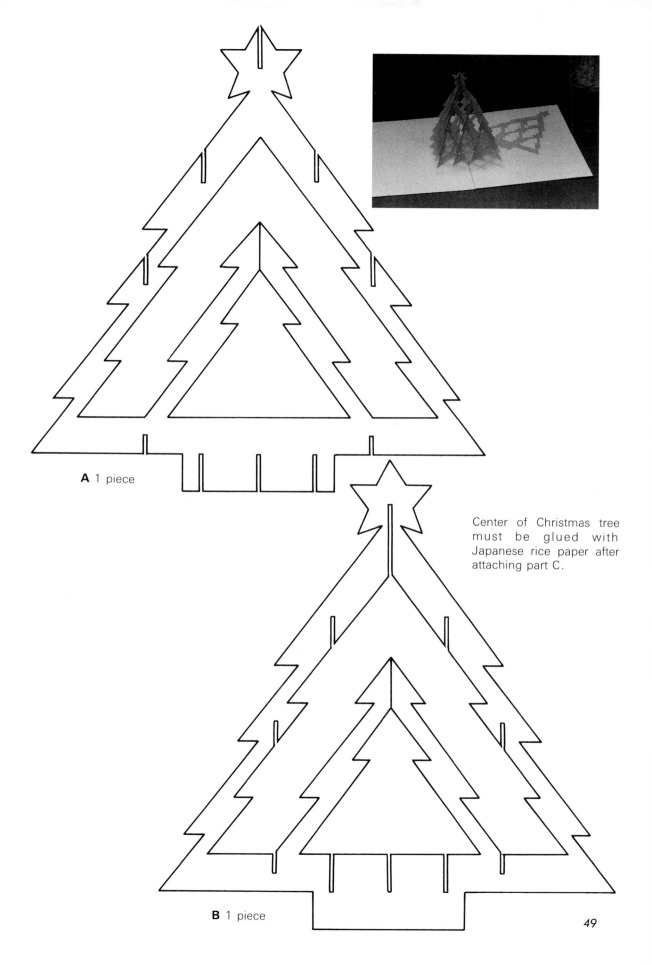

**A** 1 piece

Center of Christmas tree must be glued with Japanese rice paper after attaching part C.

**B** 1 piece

49

Base: White duna paper

Base: Colored duna paper

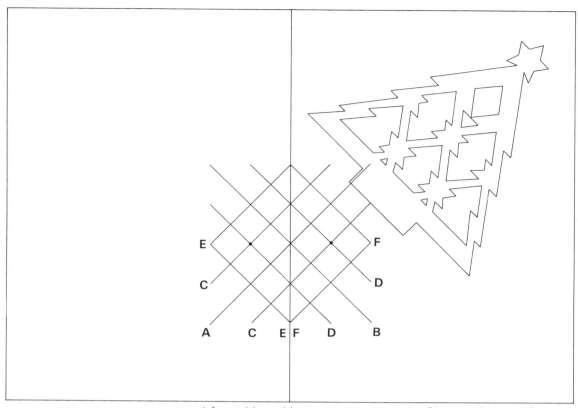

E  C  A

F  D  B

C  E|F  D

▲Assembly and base patterns are scale. Please enlarge by 2 times.

## ③ PINE, BAMBOO, and PLUM TREE (good luck symbol)

### Shown on pages 6 & 7

**Materials:**
6 Sheets white duna paper
15cm × 20cm (6″ × 8″)
3 Sheets colored duna paper
15cm × 20cm (6″ × 8″)
2 pieces Japanese rice paper
2cm × 15cm (¾″ × 6″)
Thread

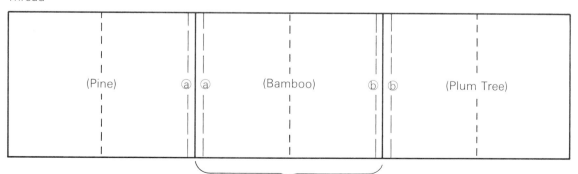

(Pine)        ⓐ ⓐ    (Bamboo)    ⓑ ⓑ    (Plum Tree)

Glue ⓐ to ⓐ and ⓑ to ⓑ with Japanese rice paper.

Attach reinforcement with colored paper.

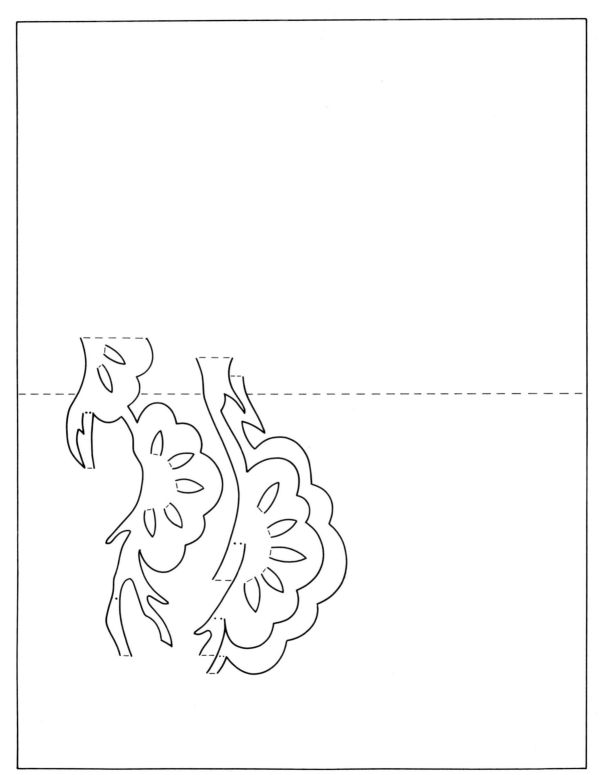

ⓐ

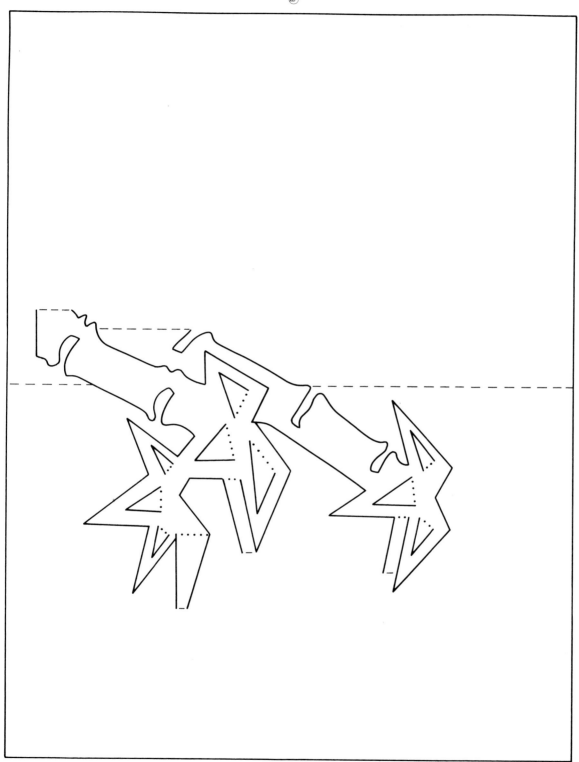

# ④ FLOWER FANTASY

### Shown on pages 6 & 7

**Materials:**

Base: 10 Sheets white Bristol paper
      15cm × 20cm (6″ × 8″)

Parts: 6 Sheets white Bristol paper
      15cm × 20cm (6″ × 8″)
      4 Sheets Bristol paper, various colors,
      15cm × 20cm (6″ × 8″)
      9 pieces Japanese rice paper
      2cm × 15 cm (34″ × 6″)

Thread

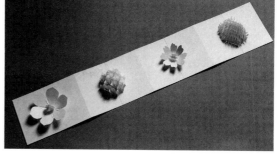

[**Chrysanthemum-Winter**]

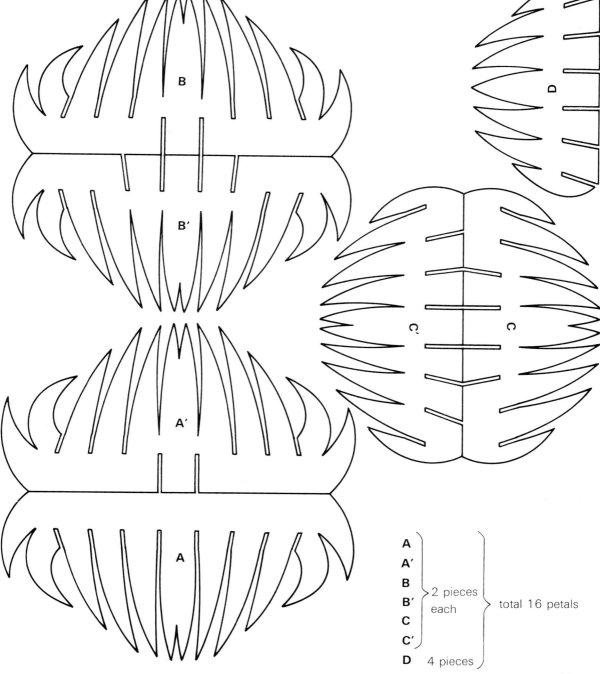

A
A′
B
B′
C
C′
} 2 pieces each
D 4 pieces
} total 16 petals

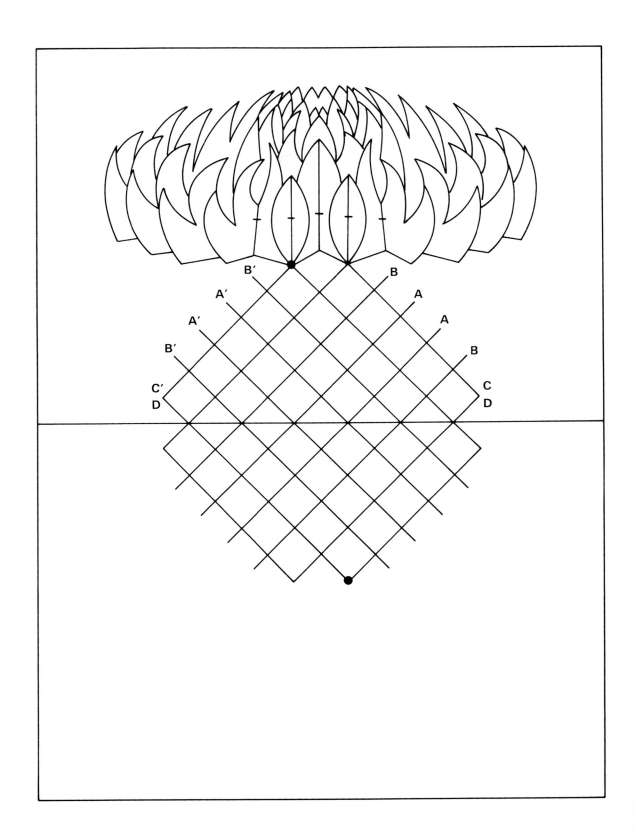

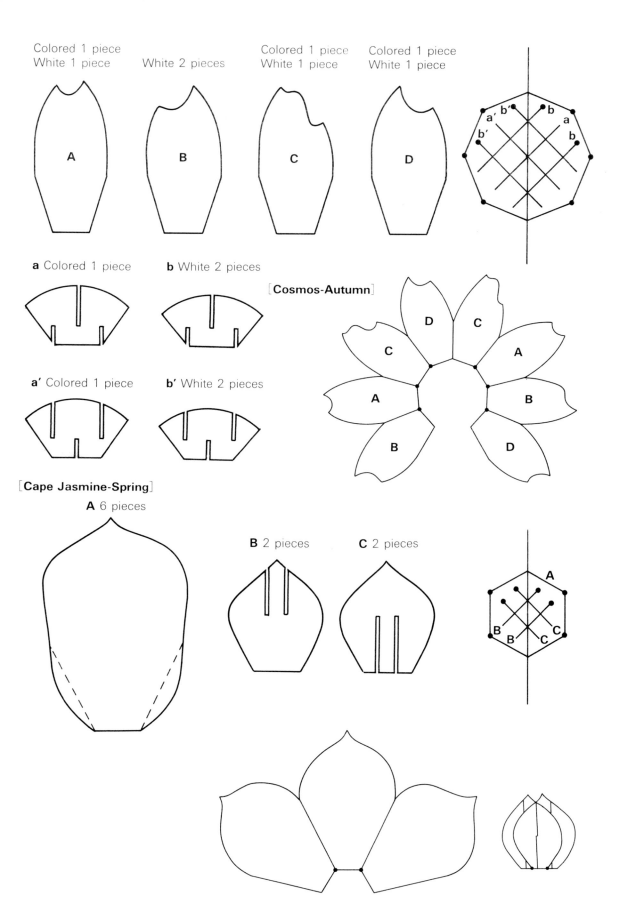

Colored 1 piece
White 1 piece

White 2 pieces

Colored 1 piece
White 1 piece

Colored 1 piece
White 1 piece

A

B

C

D

**a** Colored 1 piece

**b** White 2 pieces

[**Cosmos-Autumn**]

D    C

C        A

A        B

B        D

**a'** Colored 1 piece

**b'** White 2 pieces

[**Cape Jasmine-Spring**]

**A** 6 pieces

**B** 2 pieces

**C** 2 pieces

A

B  B    C  C

57

**[Hydrangea-Summer]**

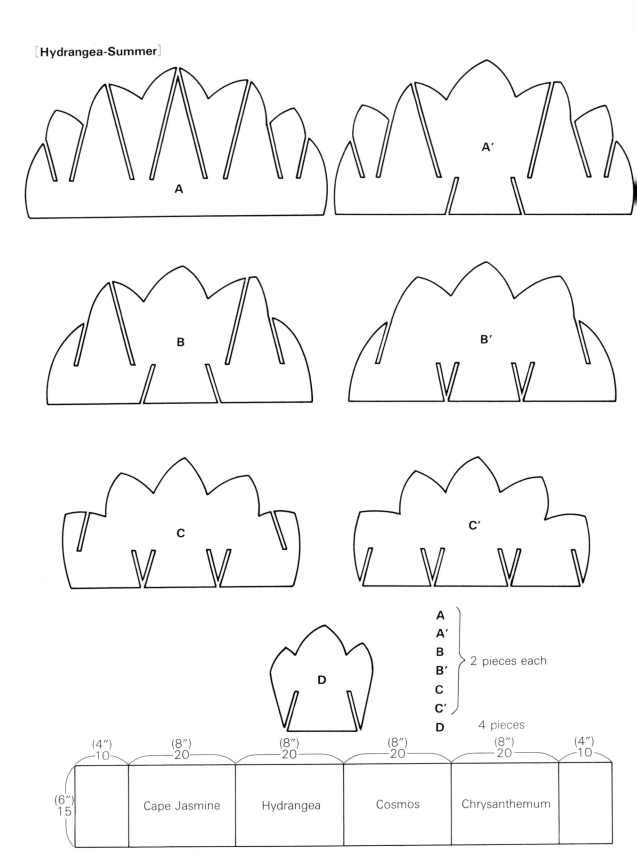

A

A′

B

B′

C

C′

D

A
A′
B
B′
C
C′ } 2 pieces each

D    4 pieces

| (4")<br>10 | (8")<br>20 | (8")<br>20 | (8")<br>20 | (8")<br>20 | (4")<br>10 |
|---|---|---|---|---|---|
| (6")<br>15 | Cape Jasmine | Hydrangea | Cosmos | Chrysanthemum | |

After placing the flowers on the base, glue them in place with Japanese rice paper before reinforcing.
Attach a 10cm × 15cm (4″ × 6″) card to each side.

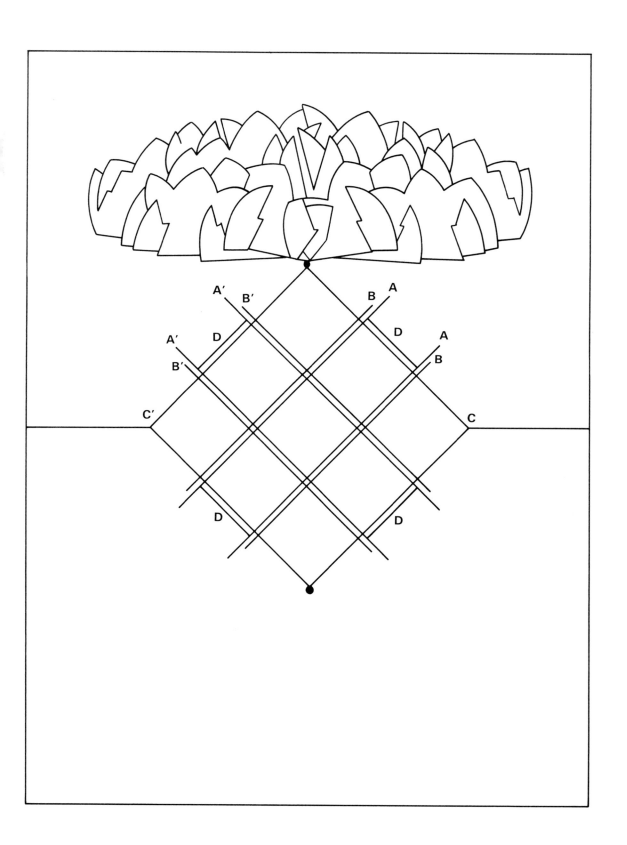

A′  B′        B  A

A′   D      D    A

B′                B

C′                        C

D              D

# ② SKIING SANTA CLAUS

### Shown on page 5

**Materials:**
2 Sheets white duna paper
30cm × 21cm (12″ × 8¼″)
6 Sheets white duna paper
16cm × 22cm (6¼″ × 8¾″)
1 Sheet red duna paper
5cm × 5cm (2″ × 2″)
Japanese rice paper
Thread

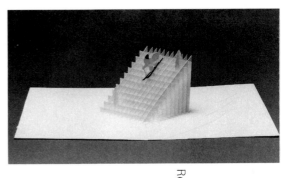

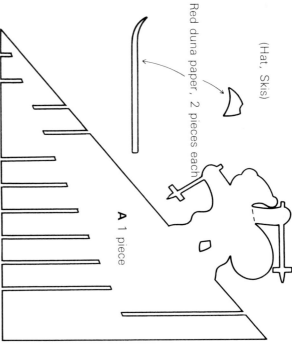

(Hat, Skis)

Red duna paper, 2 pieces each

**A** 1 piece

White duna paper

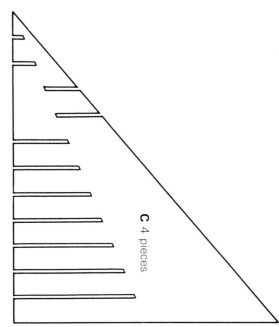

**C** 4 pieces

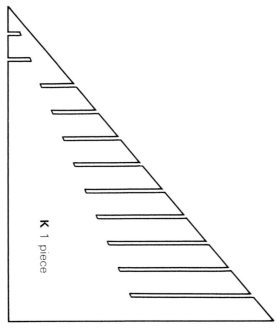

**K** 1 piece

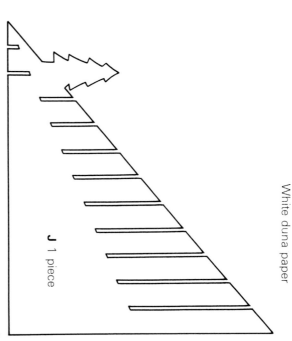

**J** 1 piece

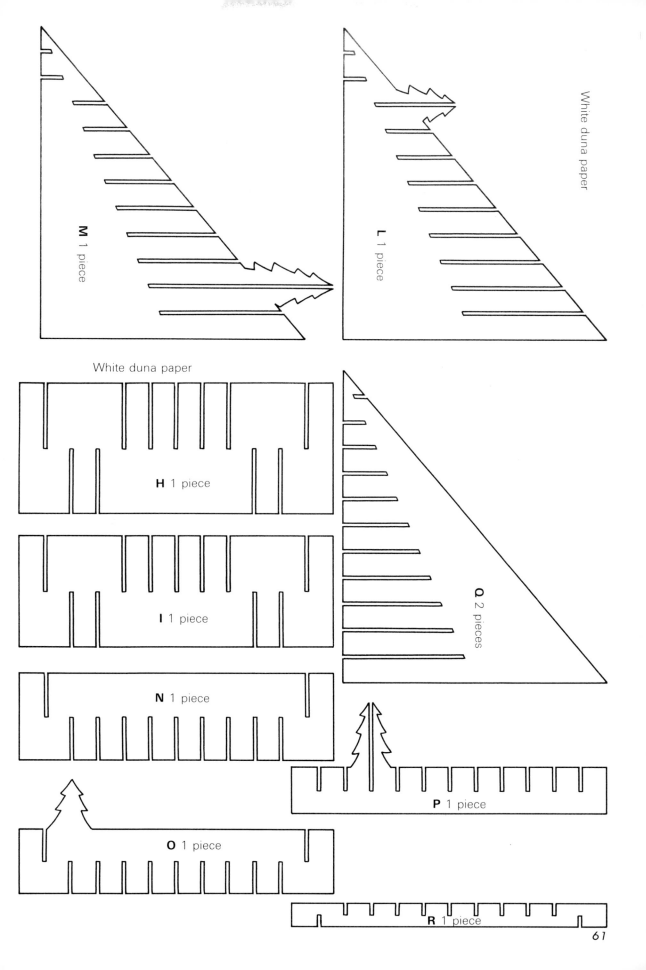

White duna paper

M 1 piece

L 1 piece

White duna paper

H 1 piece

I 1 piece

N 1 piece

Q 2 pieces

P 1 piece

O 1 piece

R 1 piece

White duna paper

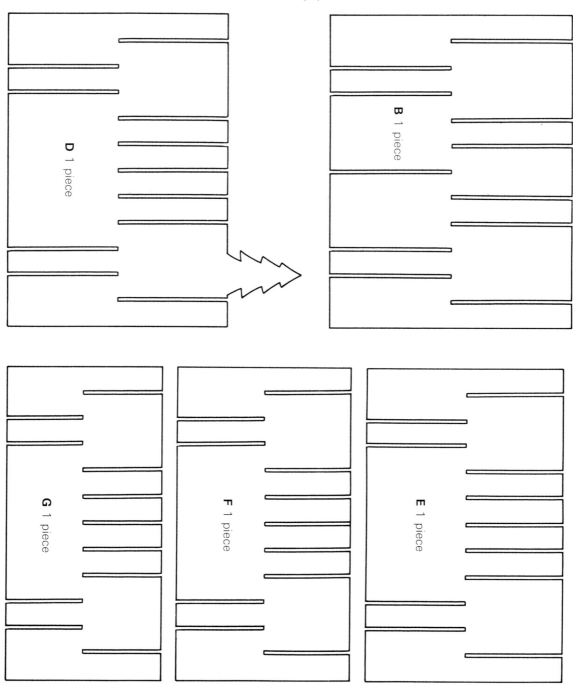

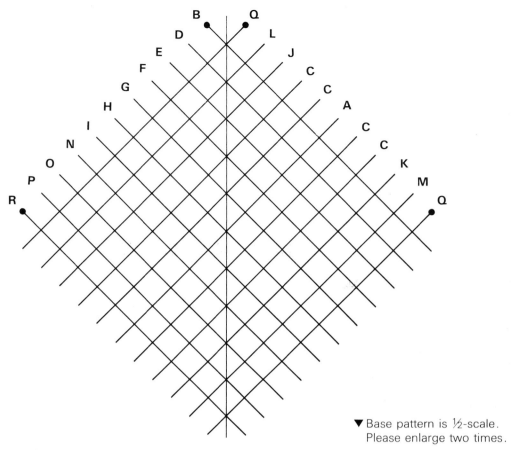

B Q
D L
E J
F C
G C
H A
I C
N C
O K
P M
R Q

▼ Base pattern is ½-scale.
Please enlarge two times.

Base White duna paper

## ⑤ MAGNOLIA  **Shown on page 8**

**Materials:**
1 Sheet white duna paper
15cm × 20cm (6″ × 8″)
1 Sheet colored duna paper
15cm × 20cm (6″ × 8″)

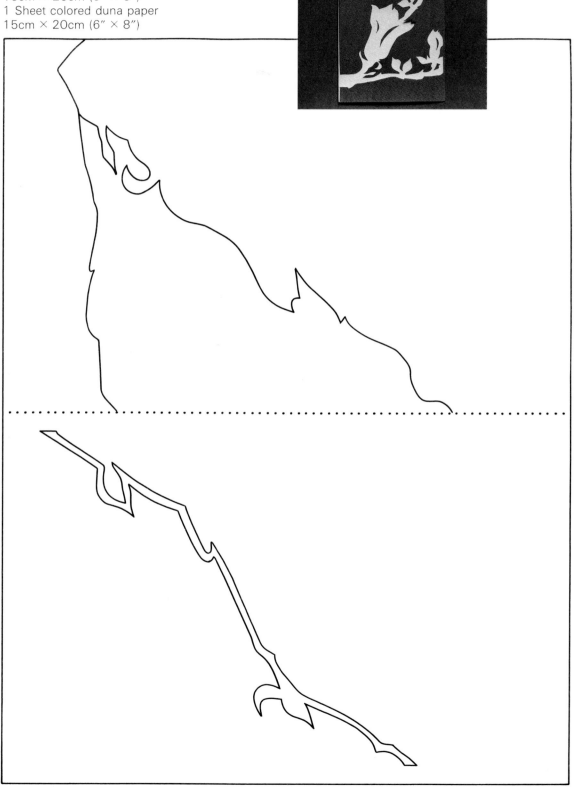

Colored

64

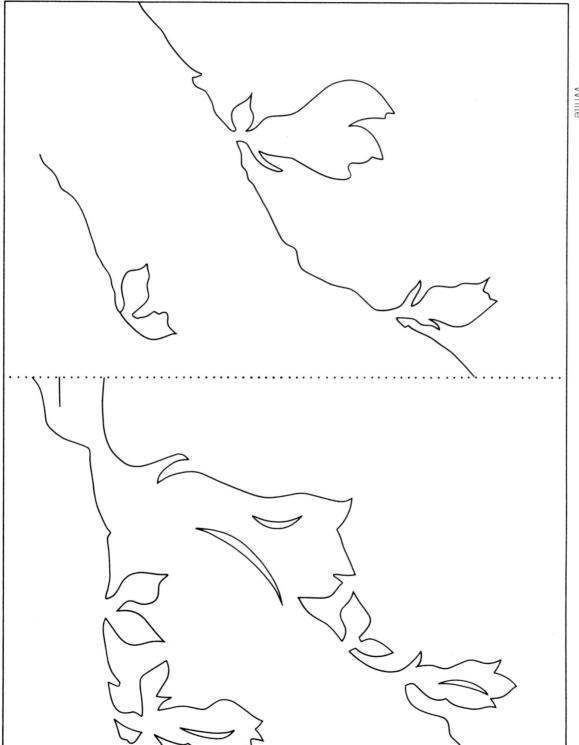

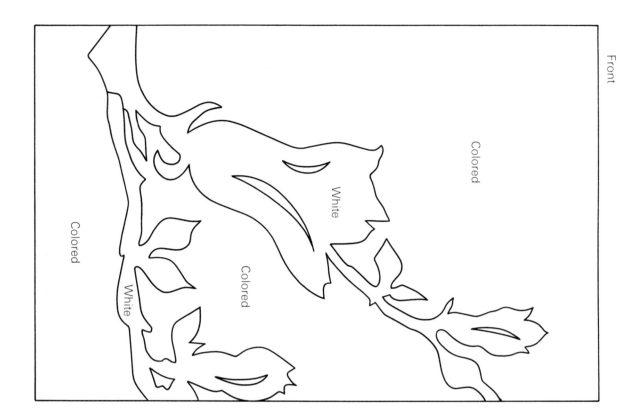

Front

Colored

Colored

White

Colored

White

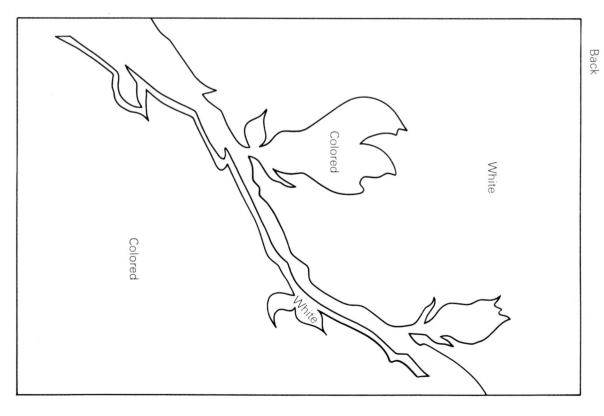

Back

White

Colored

Colored

White

# ⑥ MOUNT FUJI  Shown on page 8

**Materials:**
1 Sheet white duna paper 15cm × 20cm (6″ × 8″)
1 Sheet colored duna paper 15cm × 20cm (6″ × 8″)

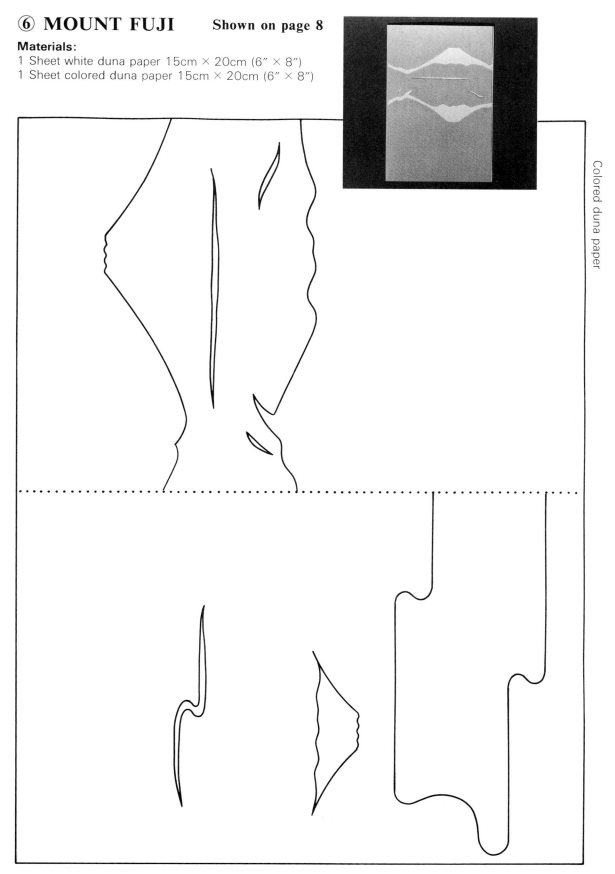

Colored duna paper

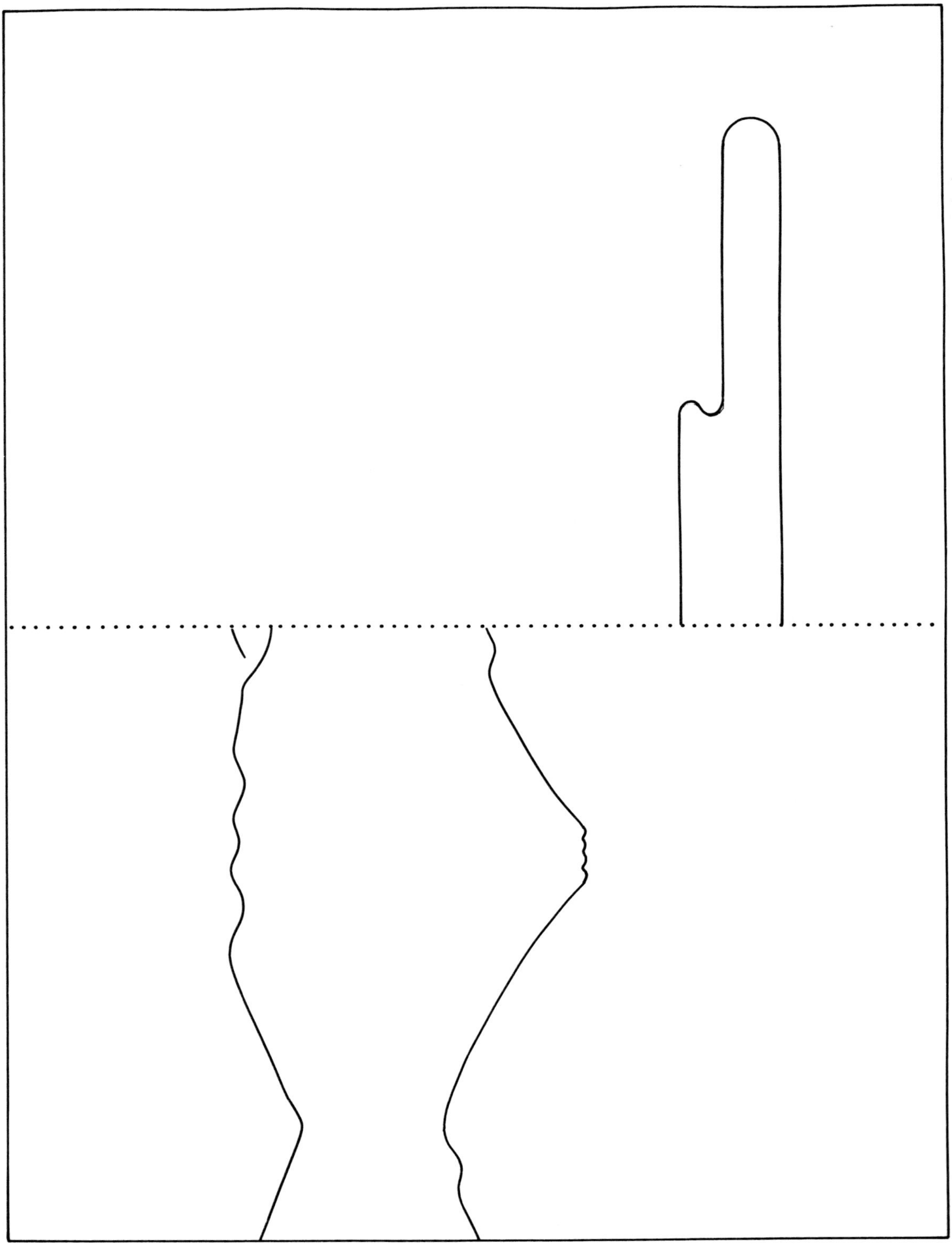

White duna paper

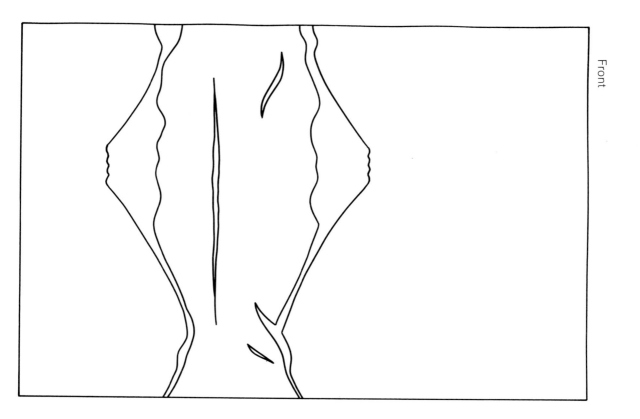

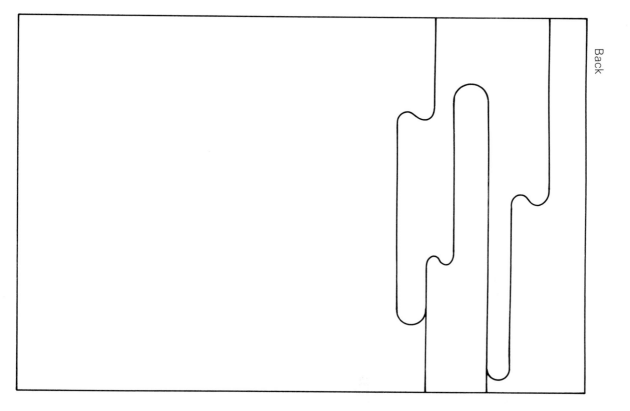

## ⑦ THISTLE  **Shown on page 8**

**Materials:**
1 Sheet white duna paper 15cm × 20cm (6″ × 8″)
1 Sheet colored duna paper 15cm × 20cm (6″ × 8″)

Colored duna paper

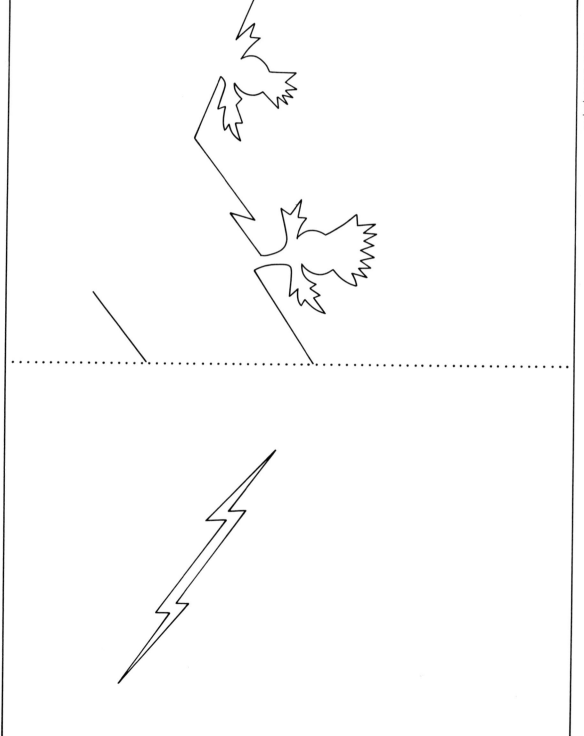

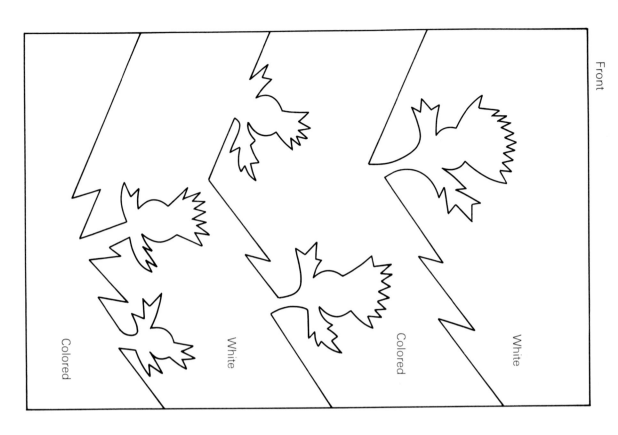

Front

Colored

White

Colored

White

## ⑧ **PLOVER**　　**Shown on page 9**

**Materials:**
1 Sheet white duna paper
15cm × 20cm (6″ × 8″)
1 Sheet colored duna paper
15cm × 20cm (6″ × 8″)
1 Sheet gold colored paper
15cm × 10cm (6″ × 4″)

Assembly Order

Diagram **A**

↓

Gold colored paper

(insert in slot)

↓

Diagram **B**

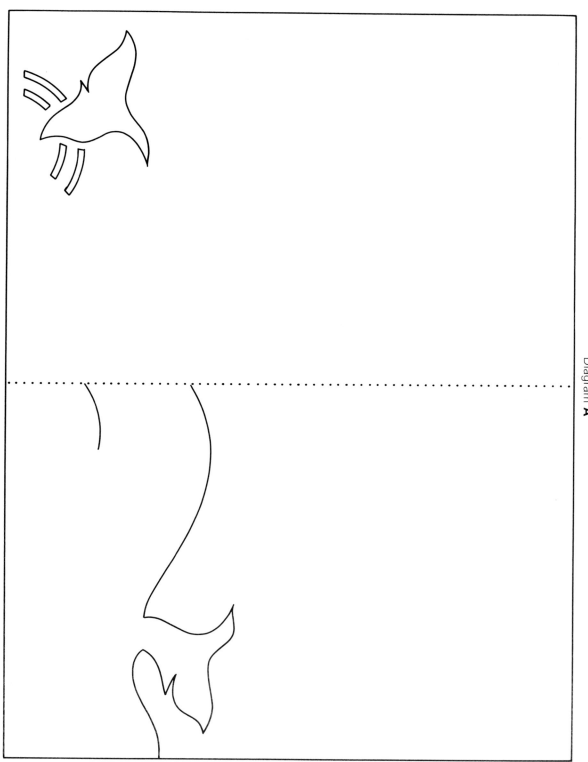

Diagram **A**

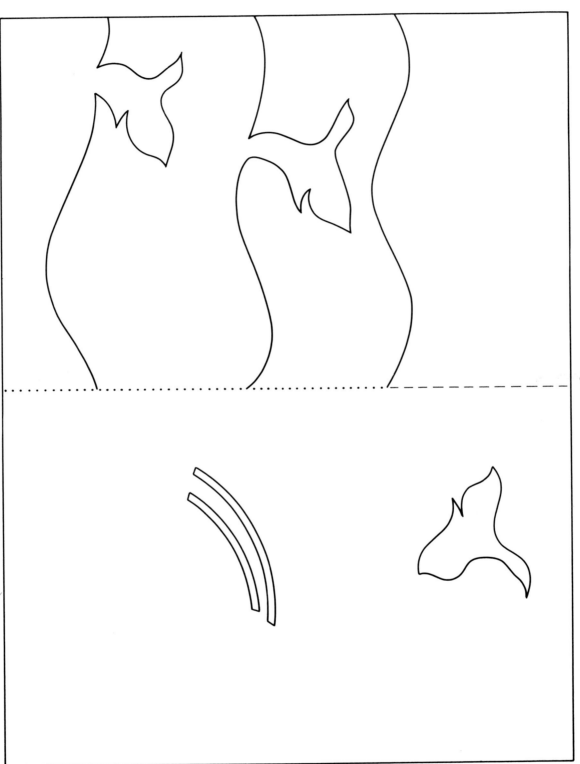

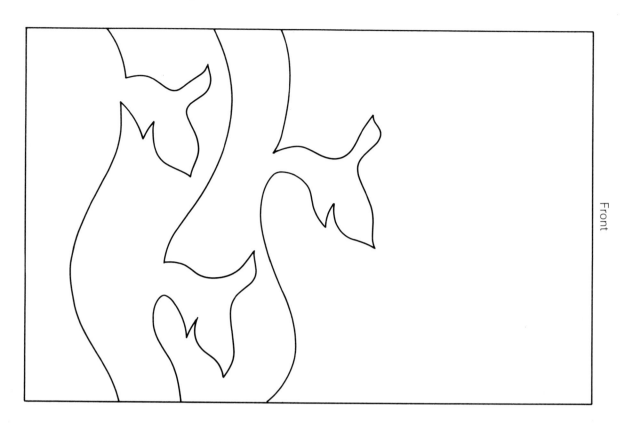

Front

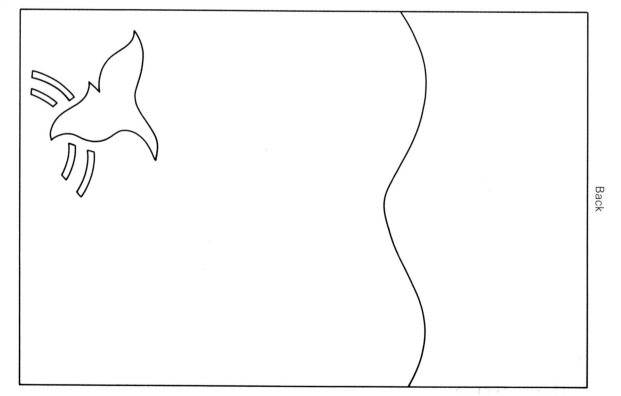

Back

⑩ **CELEBRATION CRANE**     **Shown on page 9**

Colored duna paper

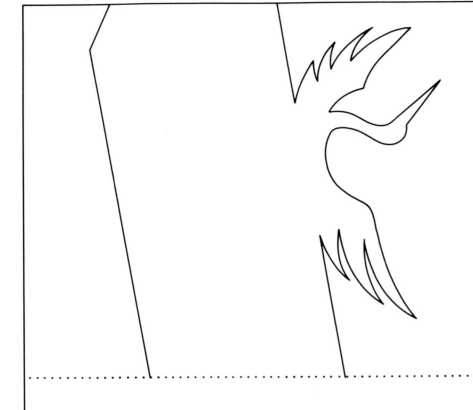

**Materials:**
1 Sheet white duna paper 15cm × 20cm (6″ × 8″)
1 Sheet colored duna paper 15cm × 20cm (6″ × 8″)

## ⑫ CAT

**Shown on page 10**

**Materials:**
2 Sheets white duna paper
12cm × 12cm (4¾″ × 4¾″)
1 Sheet colored duna paper
12cm × 12cm (4¾″ × 4¾″)

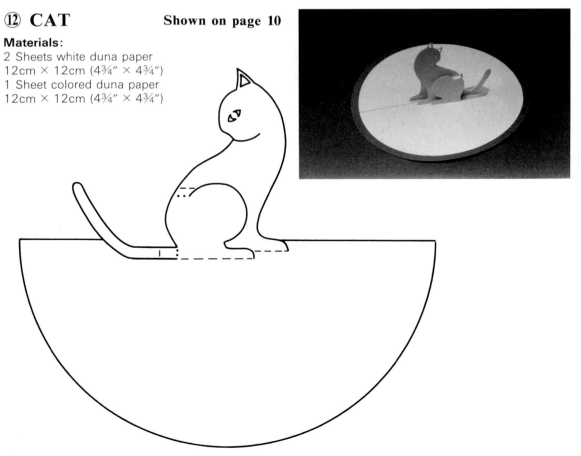

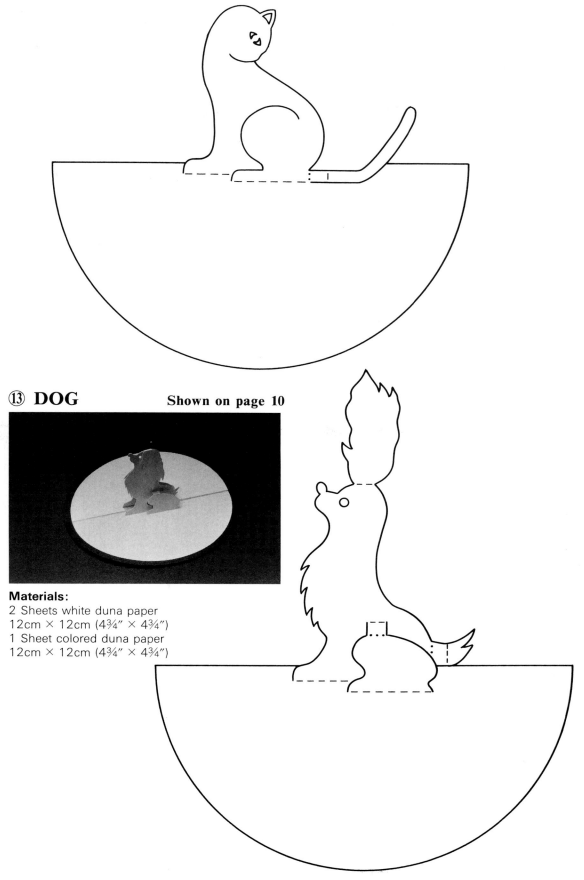

⑬ **DOG**          **Shown on page 10**

**Materials:**
2 Sheets white duna paper
12cm × 12cm (4¾″ × 4¾″)
1 Sheet colored duna paper
12cm × 12cm (4¾″ × 4¾″)

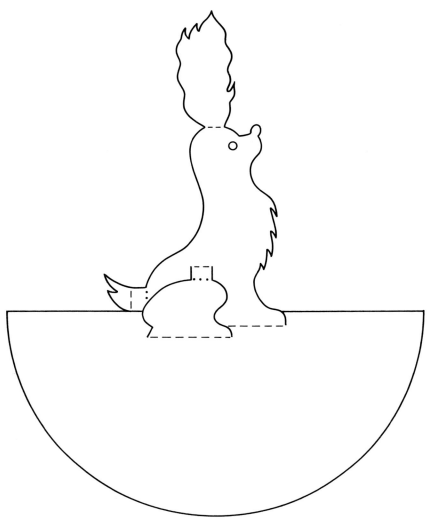

## ⑭ ANGEL WITH HEART (with ceremonial envelope)

**Shown on page 10**

**Materials:**
3 Sheets white duna paper
16cm × 19cm (6¼″ × 7½″)
1 Sheet light duna paper
20cm × 19cm (6¼″ × 7½″)
for envelope

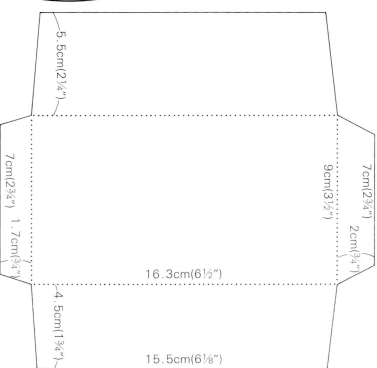

5.5cm(2¼″)

7cm(2¾″)

1.7cm(¾″)

4.5cm(1¾″)

16.3cm(6½″)

15.5cm(6⅛″)

9cm(3½″)

7cm(2¾″)

2cm(¾″)

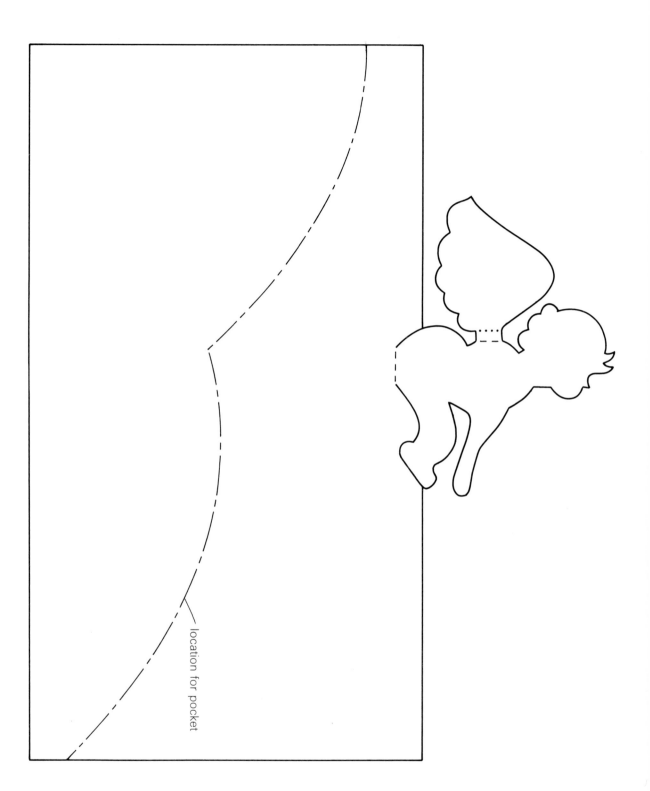

location for pocket

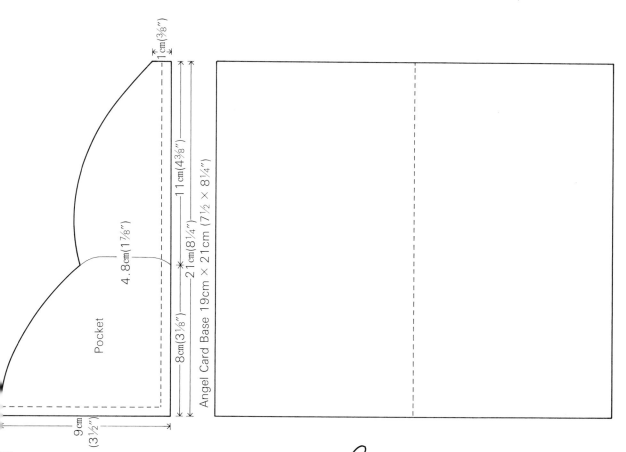

1cm (³⁄₈")

11cm (4³⁄₈")

4.8cm (1⁷⁄₈")

Pocket

8cm (3¹⁄₈")

21cm (8¼")

Angel Card Base 19cm × 21cm (7½ × 8¼")

9cm (3½")

# ⑰ CARIBOU

## Shown on page 11

**Materials:**
3 Sheets white duna paper
10cm × 20cm (4″ × 8″)

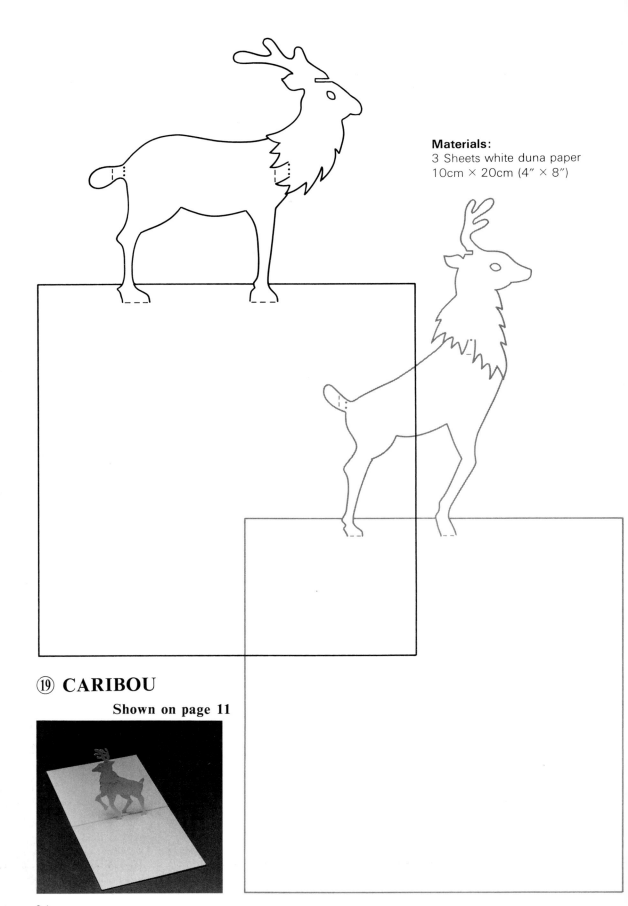

**Materials:**
3 Sheets white duna paper
10cm × 20cm (4″ × 8″)

⑲ **CARIBOU**

**Shown on page 11**

## ⑯ MINI-CHRISTMAS TREE

### Shown on page 11

**Materials:**
1 Sheet white duna paper
18cm × 5.5cm (7″ × 2¼″)
1 Sheet colored duna paper
18cm × 5.5cm (7 × 2¼″)

※ Place a star sticker at the top of the tree.

# ⑪⑮ COLT IN A SPRING FIELD
## (Red and White)
### Shown on pages 10 & 11

**Materials:**
Parts: 1 Sheet white duna paper
          10cm × 15cm (4" × 6")
       1 Sheet colored duna paper
          10cm × 15cm (4" × 6")
Base: 1 Sheet white duna paper
          11.5cm × 23cm (4½" × 9")
       1 Sheet colored duna paper
          11.5cm × 19cm (4½" × 7½")
Japanese rice paper
Thread

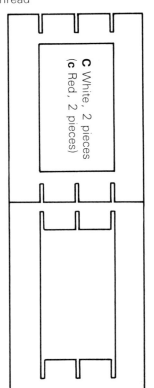

C White, 2 pieces
(c Red, 2 pieces)

E White, 4 pieces
(e Red, 4 pieces)

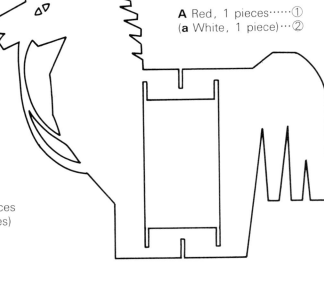

A Red, 1 pieces······①
(a White, 1 piece)···②

D White, 2 pieces
(d Red, 2 pieces)

B Red, 1 piece
(b White 1 piece)

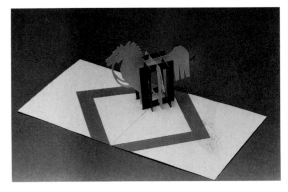

※ This craft is just the opposite color. Try to make both of them. There should be no problem with the parts, since they are thesame sizes. Make sure to make the base in the opposite colors, too.

Red

White

Red

Red

White

Red

E D
A
E D
C E
B
C E

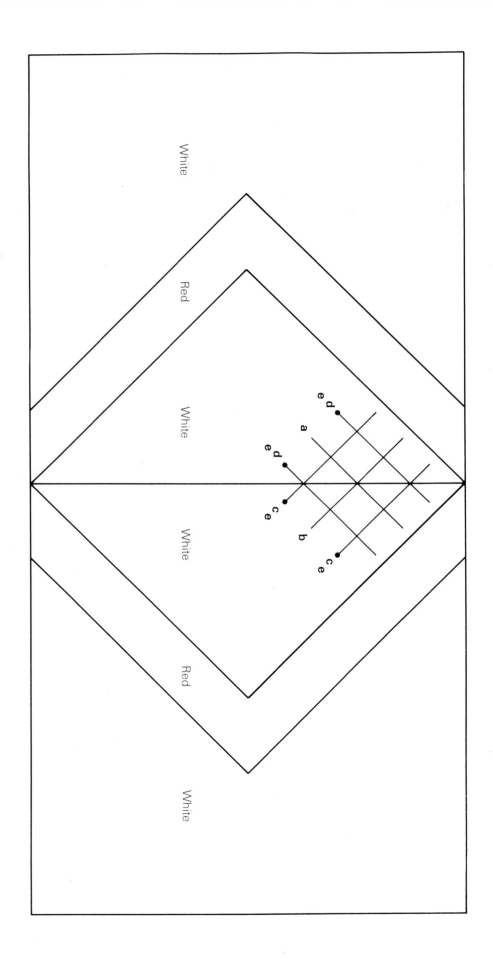

Base { White duna paper 11.5cm × 23cm (4½" × 9")......①
Base { Red duna paper 11.5cm × 23cm (4½" × 9")......②

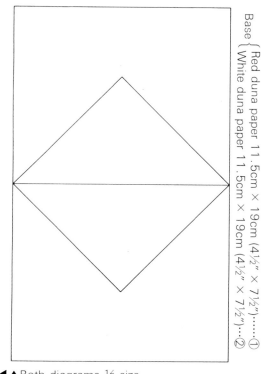

Base { Red duna paper 11.5cm × 19cm (4½" × 7½")......①
Base { White duna paper 11.5cm × 19cm (4½" × 7½")......②

◀▲Both diagrams ½-size

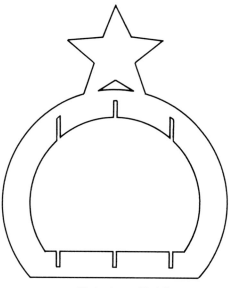

## ㉖ STAR    Shown on page 14

**Materials:**
3 Sheets white duna paper 15cm × 20cm (6" × 8")
2 Sheets gold colored duna paper
15cm × 20cm (6" × 8")
Japanese rice paper
Thread

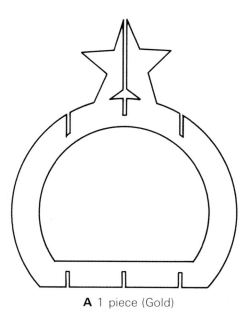

**A** 1 piece (Gold)          **B** 1 piece (Gold)

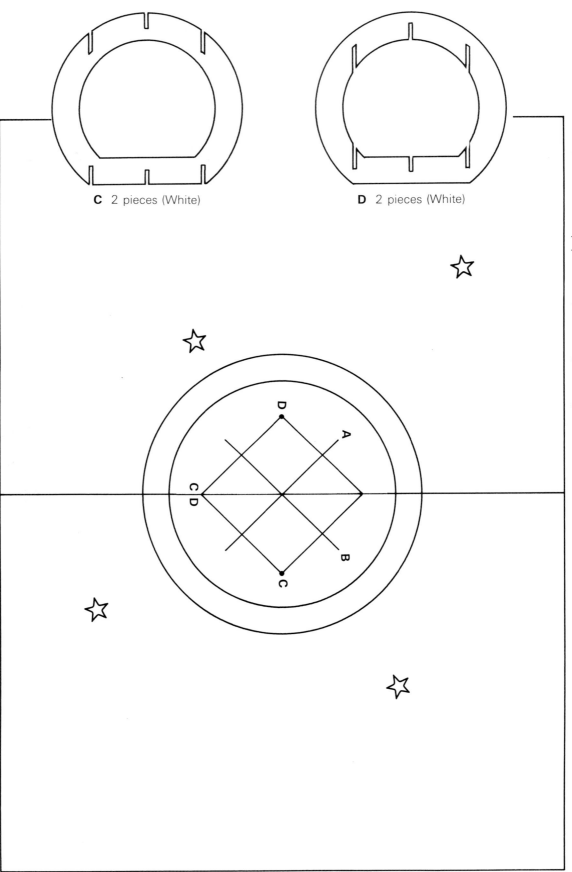

**C** 2 pieces (White)

**D** 2 pieces (White)

## ㉙ GIFT BOX  **Shown on page 15**

**Materials:**
3 Sheets white duna paper 15cm × 20cm (6″ × 8″)
1 Sheet colored duna paper 15cm × 20cm (6″ × 8″)
Japanese rice paper
Thread

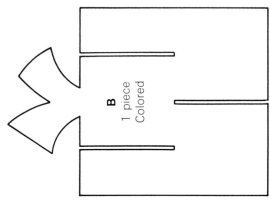

**B**
1 piece
Colored

**D**
4 pieces
White

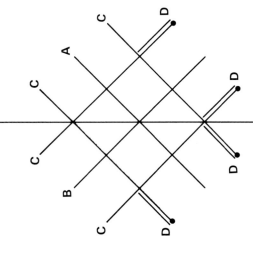

C
A
D
C
D
C
D
B
D
C
D

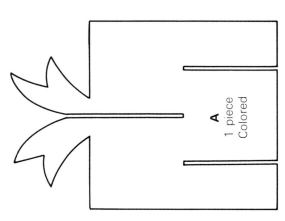

**A**
1 piece
Colored

**C**
4 pieces
White

## (27)(30) ROUND BOW
### Shown on pages 14 & 15

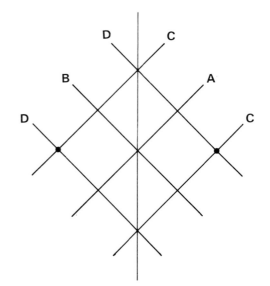

**Materials:**
1 Sheet white duna paper 15cm × 20cm (6″ × 8″)
2 Sheets red duna paper 15cm × 20cm (6″ × 8″)
1 Sheet green duna paper 15cm × 20cm (6″ × 8″)
Japanese rice paper
Thread

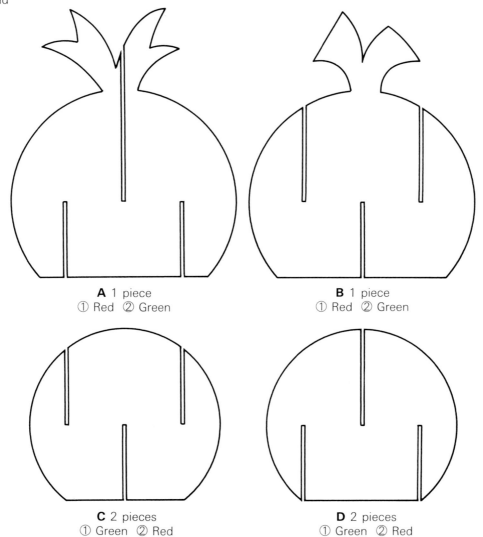

**A** 1 piece
① Red  ② Green

**B** 1 piece
① Red  ② Green

**C** 2 pieces
① Green  ② Red

**D** 2 pieces
① Green  ② Red

Red

White

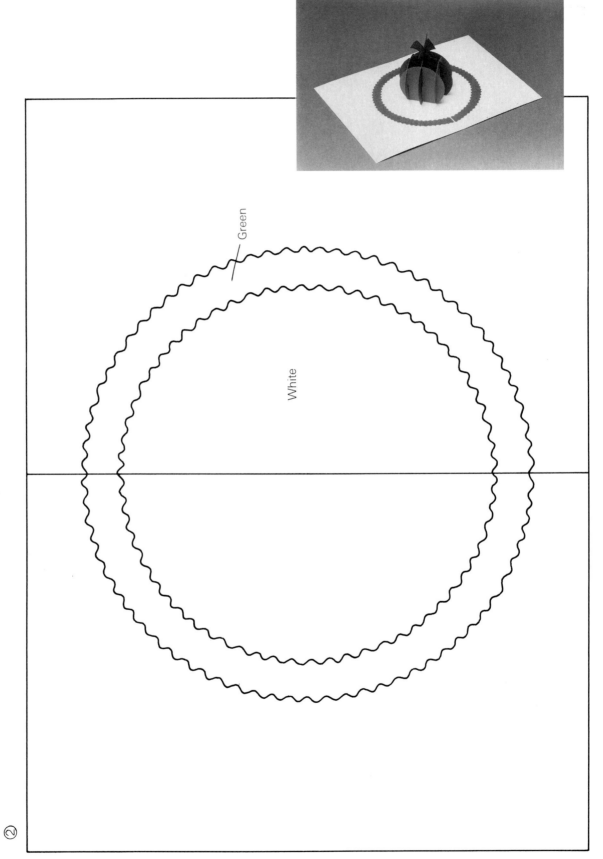

Green

White

②

94

**E** 1 piece
Green

# ㉘ TULIP IN GLOBE

**Shown on page 15**

**Materials:**
3 Sheets white duna paper 15cm × 20cm (6″ × 8″)
1 Sheet colored duna paper 15cm × 20cm (6″ × 8″)
Japanese rice paper
Thread

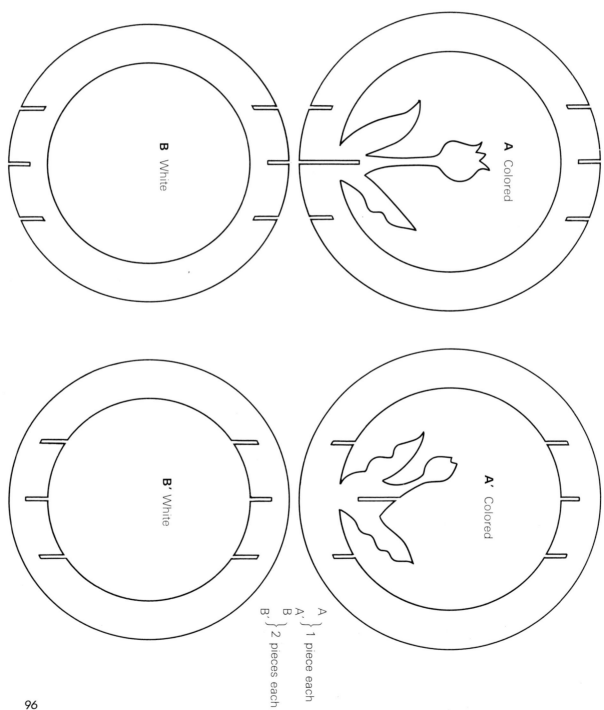

B White

A Colored

B' White

A' Colored

A'
A  } 1 piece each
B
B' } 2 pieces each

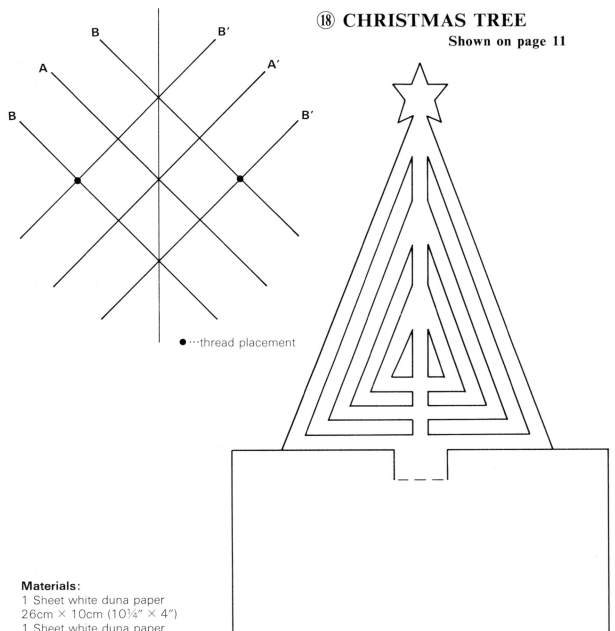

● ···thread placement

**Materials:**
1 Sheet white duna paper
26cm × 10cm (10¼" × 4")
1 Sheet white duna paper
15cm × 10cm (6" × 4")
1 Sheet colored duna paper
30cm × 10cm (12" × 4")

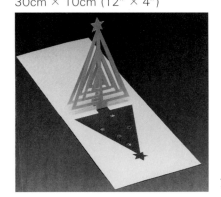

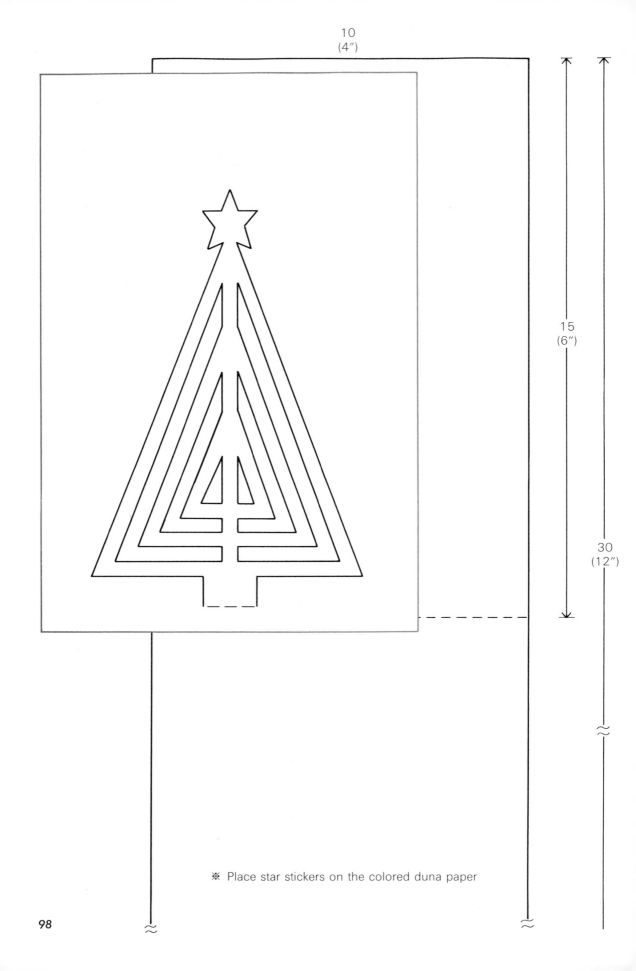

10
(4")

15
(6")

30
(12")

※ Place star stickers on the colored duna paper

# ㊳ FLOWER BASKET

### Shown on page 18

A

**Materials:**
5 Sheets white duna paper
15cm × 20cm (6″ × 8″)
1 Sheet colored duna paper
15cm × 20cm (6″ × 8″)
Japanese rice paper, Thread

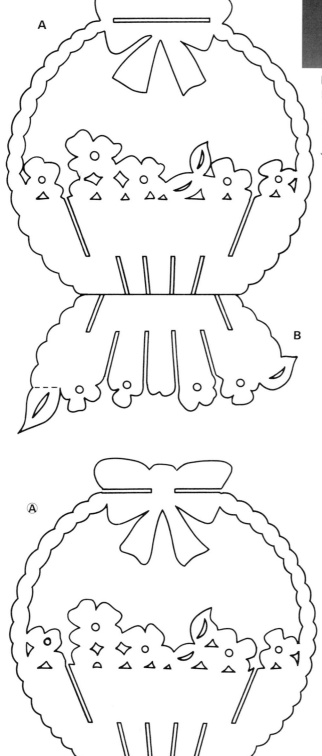

B

Ⓐ

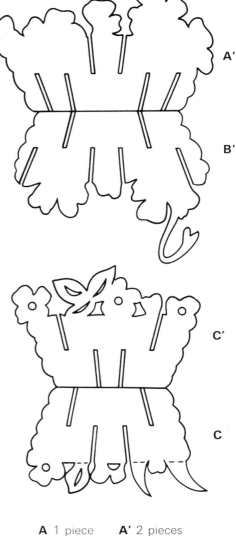

A′

B′

C′

C

| | |
|---|---|
| **A** 1 piece | **A′** 2 pieces |
| Ⓐ 1 piece | |
| **B** 2 pieces | **B′** 2 pieces |
| **C** 2 pieces | **C′** 2 pieces |

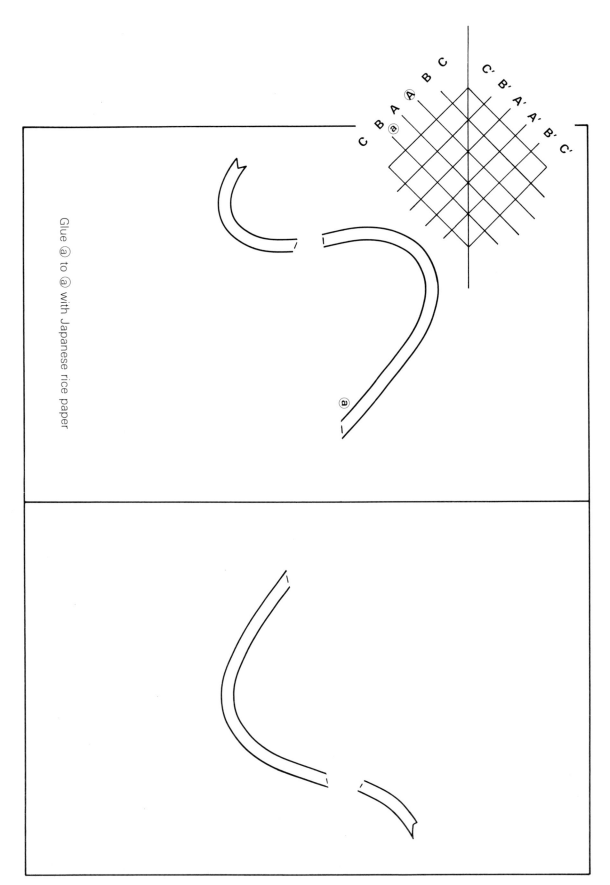

Glue ⓐ to ⓐ with Japanese rice paper

C B A Ⓐ B C     C' B' A' A' B' C'

# ㊵ FLOWER GARDEN
## Shown on page 18

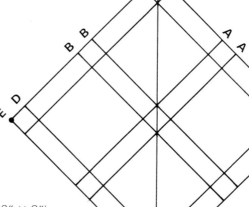

**Materials:**
3 Sheets white Bristol paper 15cm × 20cm (6″ × 8″)
1 Sheet colored Bristol paper 15cm × 20cm (6″ × 8″)
Japanese rice paper
Thread

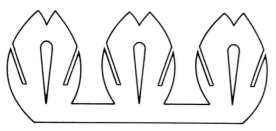

**A** Colored Bristol paper 1 piece
**A** White Bristol paper  1 piece
**F** White Bristol paper  2 pieces

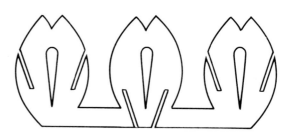

**C** White Bristol paper 2 pieces

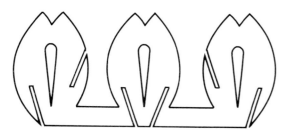

**B** Colored Bristol paper 1 piece
**B** White Bristol paper  1 piece

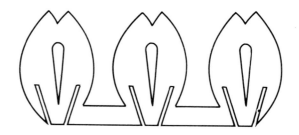

**D** White Bristol paper 2 pieces
**E** White Bristol paper 2 pieces

# ㊴ BOUQUET Shown on page 18

**Materials:**
6 Sheets white Bristol paper 15cm × 20cm (6″ × 8″)
Japanese rice paper
Thread

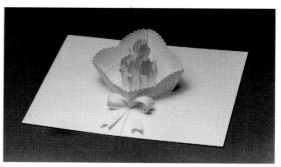

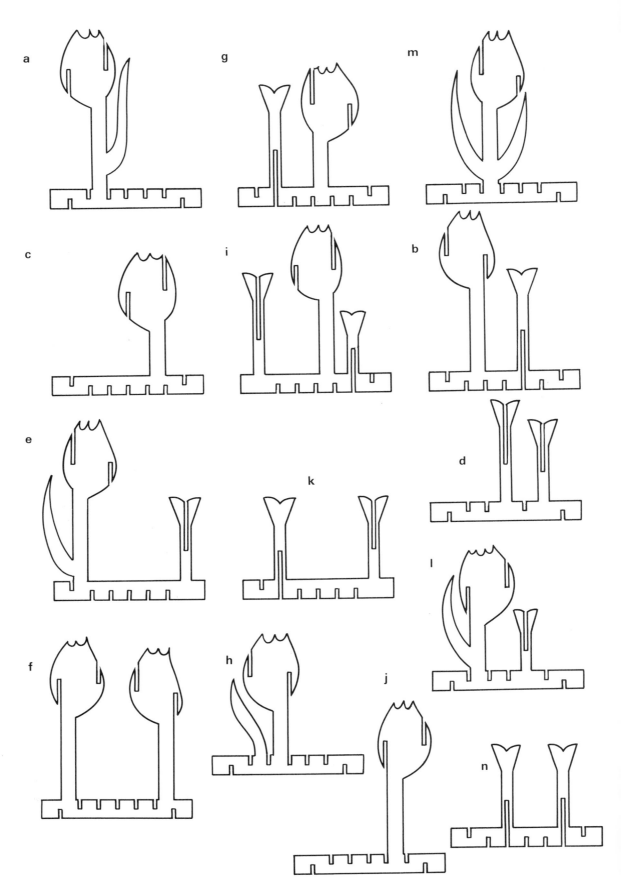

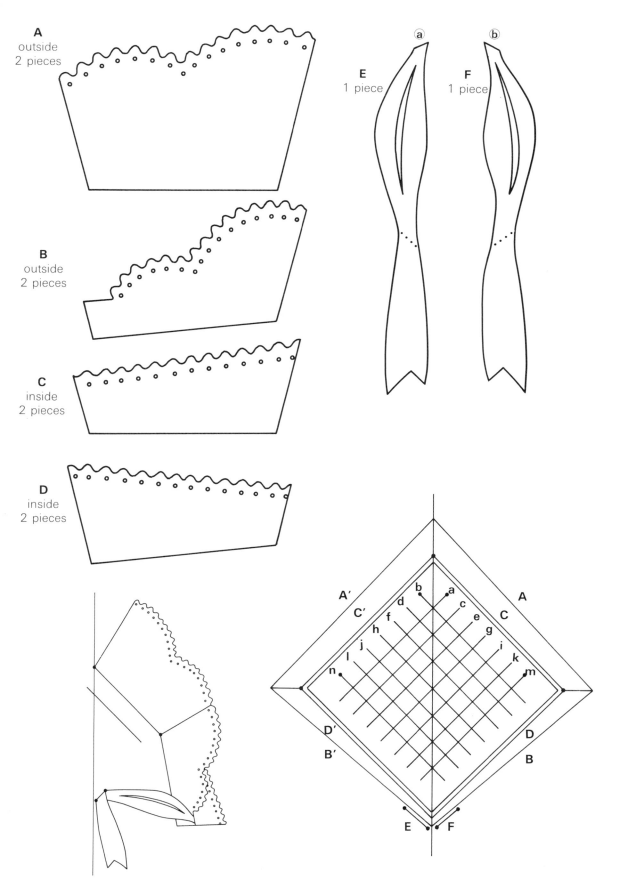

**A**
outside
2 pieces

**B**
outside
2 pieces

**C**
inside
2 pieces

**D**
inside
2 pieces

ⓐ

ⓑ

**E**
1 piece

**F**
1 piece

A'
C'
b
a
d
c
f
e
h
g
j
i
l
k
n
m
D'
D
B'
B
A
C
E
F

103

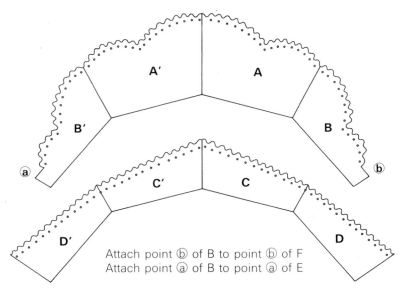

Attach point ⓑ of B to point ⓑ of F
Attach point ⓐ of B to point ⓐ of E

## ㊽ THANK YOU
### Shown on page 20

**Materials:**
1 Sheet white duna paper 16cm × 16cm
(6¼" × 6¼")
1 Sheet colored duna paper
16cm × 16cm
(6¼" × 6¼")

**Materials:**
1 Sheet colored Bristol paper
15cm × 20cm (6″ × 8″)

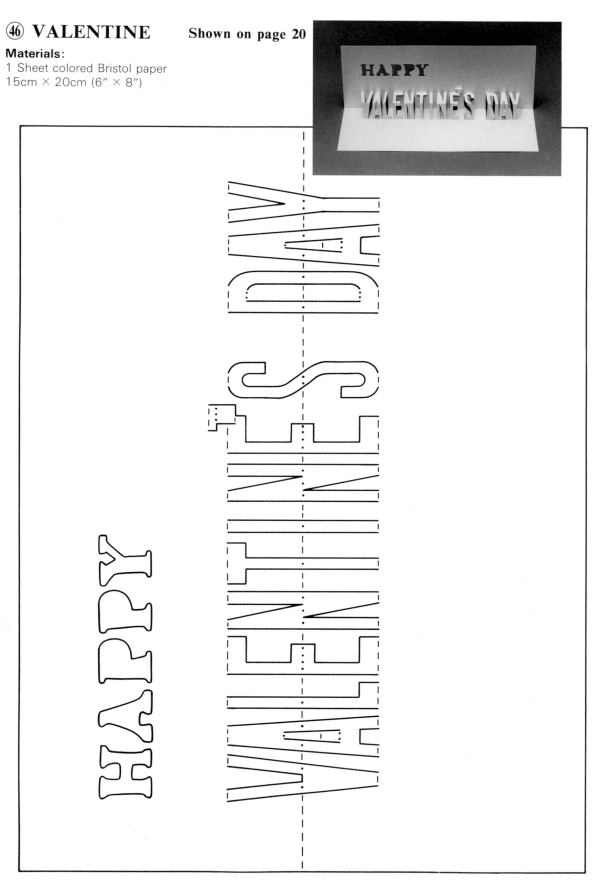

# ㊼ ANNIVERSARY CARD

## Shown on page 20

**Materials:**
1 Sheet white bristol paper 15cm × 20cm (6″ × 8″)
1 Sheet colored bristol paper 15cm × 20cm (6″ × 8″)

# ㊾ MOTHER'S DAY CARD

## Shown on page 20

**Materials:**
1 Sheet white duna paper 10.5cm × 20cm (4¼″ × 8″)
1 Sheet colored duna paper 13cm × 20cm (5¼″ × 8″)

## ㉒ GOOD LUCK SYMBOLS ON TURTLE'S BACK (longevity)

### Shown on page 12

**Materials:**
1 Sheet white duna paper 15cm × 20cm (6″ × 8″)
1 Sheet colored duna paper 15cm × 20cm (6″ × 8″)

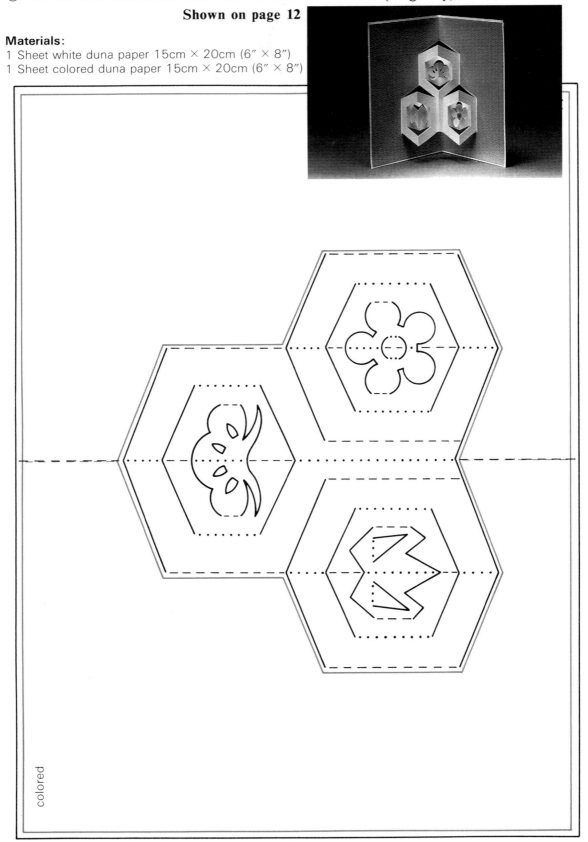

colored

# ㉕ ROUND RICE CAKES

### Shown on page 13

**Materials:**
1 Sheet white duna paper 15cm × 20cm (6″ × 8″)
1 Sheet  duna paper 15cm × 20cm (6″ × 8″)

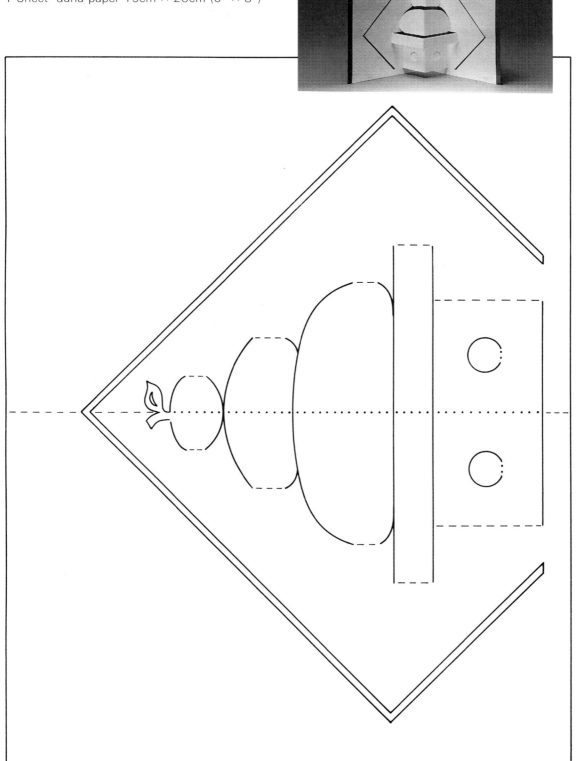

# ㉑ WEDDING BELL

### Shown on page 12

**Materials:**
1 Sheet white Bristol paper 15cm × 20cm (6″ × 8″)
1 Sheet colored Bristol paper 15cm × 20cm (6″ × 8″)

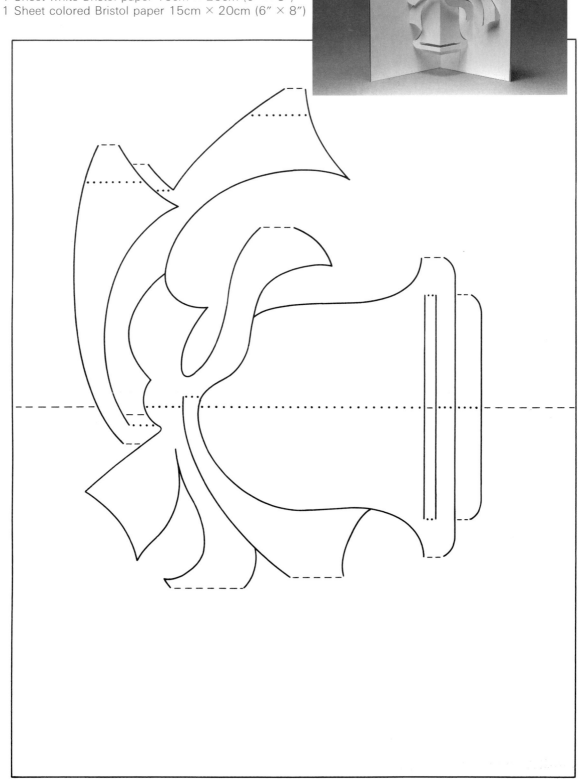

## ㉔ DANCING CRANE

### Shown on page 13

**Materials:**
2 Sheets white duna paper 15cm × 20cm (6″ × 8″)
1 Sheet colored duna paper 15cm × 20cm (6″ × 8″)

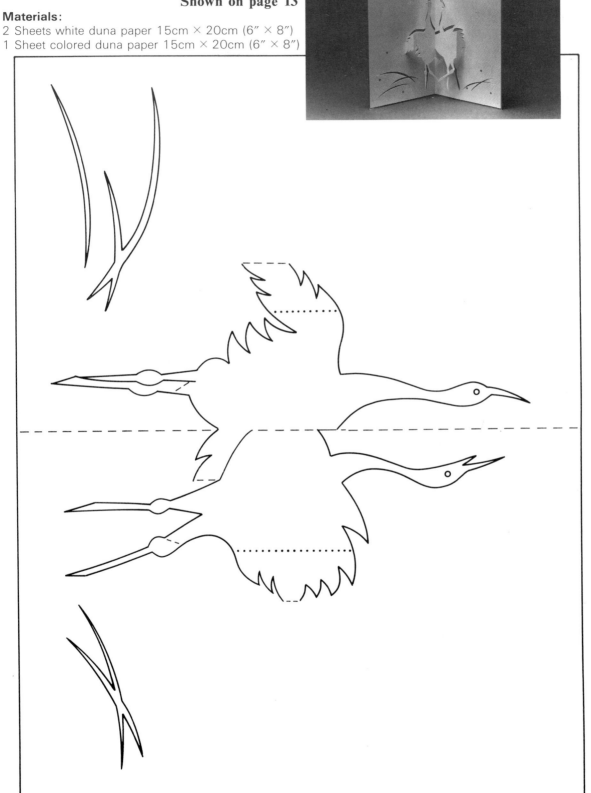

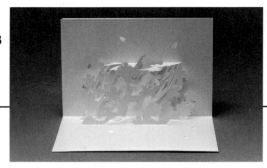

**Shown on page 13**

**Materials:**
1 Sheet colored Bristol paper
15cm × 20cm (6″ × 8″)

## ㊱ BUTTERFLY   **Shown on page 17**

**Materials:**
4 Sheets white duna paper 15cm × 20cm (6" × 8")
2 Sheets white duna paper 26cm × 21cm (10¼" × 8¼")
2 Sheets heavy, white duna paper 26cm × 21cm (10¼" × 8¼")
1 Sheet gold colored paper 26cm × 20cm (10¼" × 8")
2 Pieces Gold ribbon 30cm (12")
Japanese rice paper
Thread

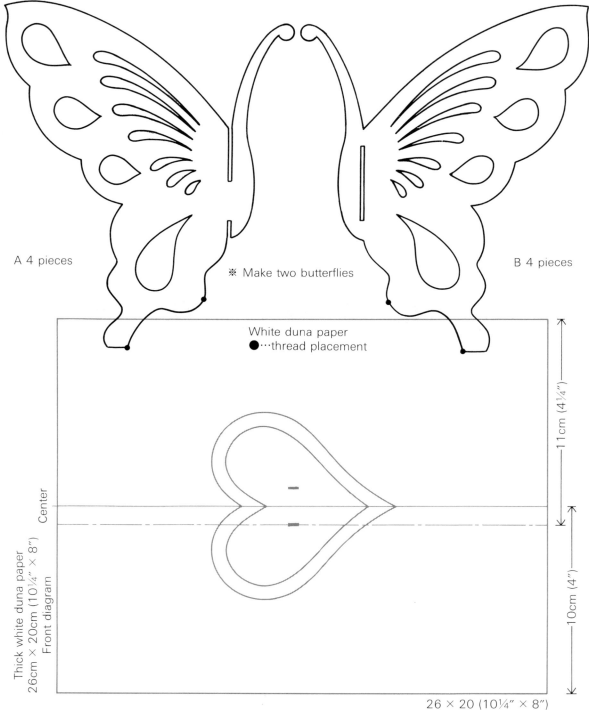

A 4 pieces

B 4 pieces

※ Make two butterflies

White duna paper
●…thread placement

Center

Thick white duna paper
26cm × 20cm (10¼" × 8")
Front diagram

11cm (4¼")

10cm (4")

26 × 20 (10¼" × 8")

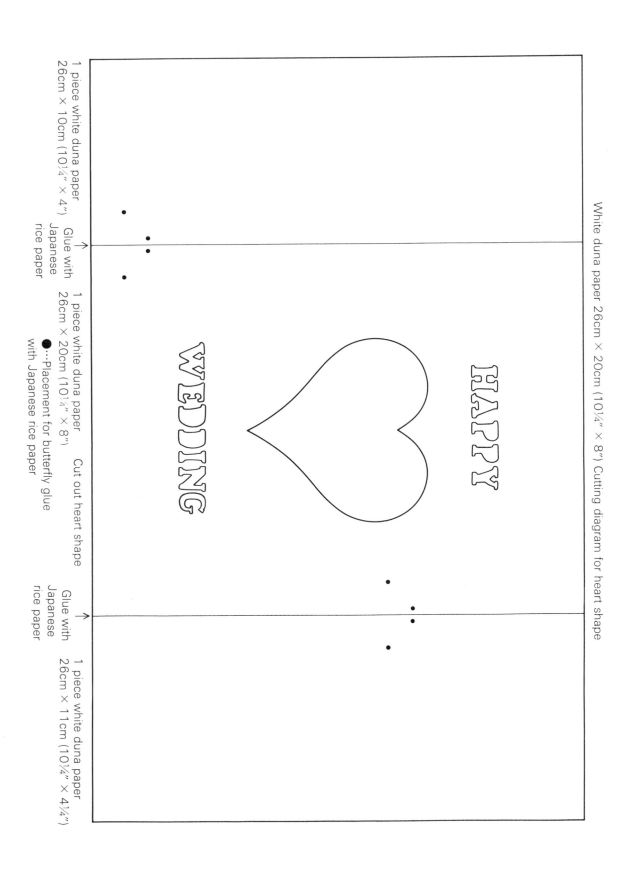

White duna paper 26cm × 20cm (10¼" × 8") Cutting diagram for heart shape

1 piece white duna paper
26cm × 10cm (10¼" × 4")

Glue with
Japanese
rice paper

1 piece white duna paper
26cm × 20cm (10¼" × 8")

Cut out heart shape

●…Placement for butterfly glue
with Japanese rice paper

Glue with
Japanese
rice paper

1 piece white duna paper
26cm × 11cm (10¼" × 4¼")

HAPPY

WEDING

## ㉟ FLOWER (Fancy Card)

### Shown on page 17

**Materials:**
1 Sheet colored duna paper 10cm × 15cm(4″ × 6″)
2 Sheets white duna paper 20cm × 21cm(8″ × 8¼″)
1 Sheet white duna paper 10cm × 15cm(4″ × 6″)
2 Sheets thick duna paper 20cm × 21cm(8″ × 8¼″)
1 Sheet pink paper 20cm × 20cm (8″ × 8″)
2 Silver ribbons 30cm (12″)
Japanese rice paper
Thread

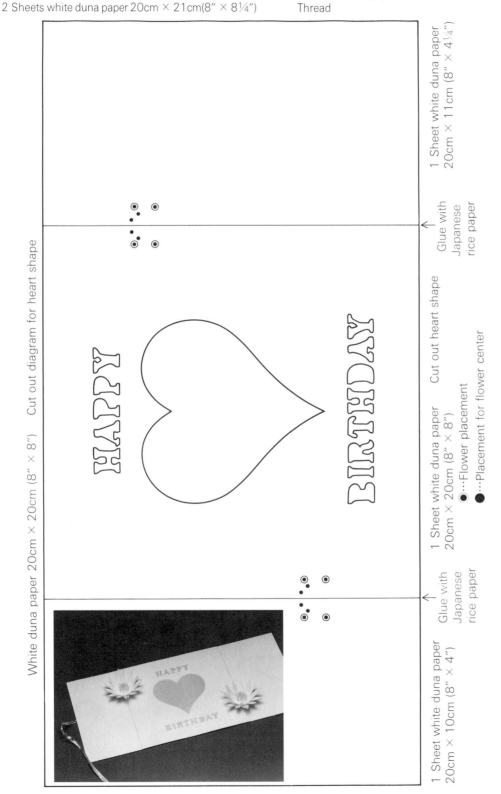

1 Sheet white duna paper 20cm × 11cm (8″ × 4¼″)

Glue with Japanese rice paper

Cut out heart shape

1 Sheet white duna paper 20cm × 20cm (8″ × 8″)

●‥‥Flower placement
●‥‥Placement for flower center

White duna paper 20cm × 20cm (8″ × 8″)    Cut out diagram for heart shape

HAPPY

BIRTHDAY

Glue with Japanese rice paper

1 Sheet white duna paper 20cm × 10cm (8″ × 4″)

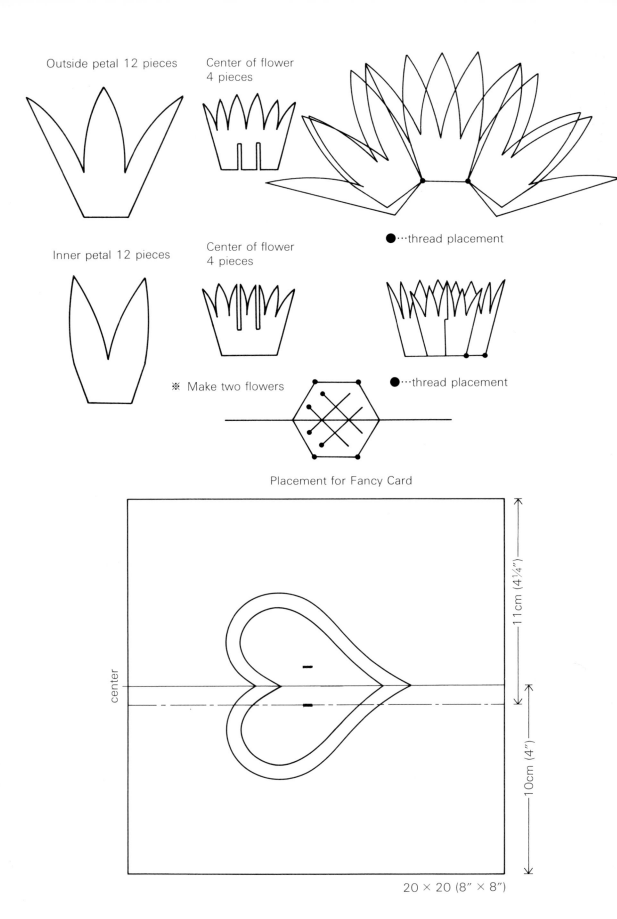

Outside petal 12 pieces

Center of flower
4 pieces

●···thread placement

Inner petal 12 pieces

Center of flower
4 pieces

●···thread placement

※ Make two flowers

Placement for Fancy Card

center

11cm (4¼")

10cm (4")

20 × 20 (8" × 8")

**Materials:**
2 Sheets white
duna paper
24cm × 27cm
(9½″ × 10¾″)
1 Sheet colored
duna paper
24cm × 27cm
(9½″ × 10¾″)

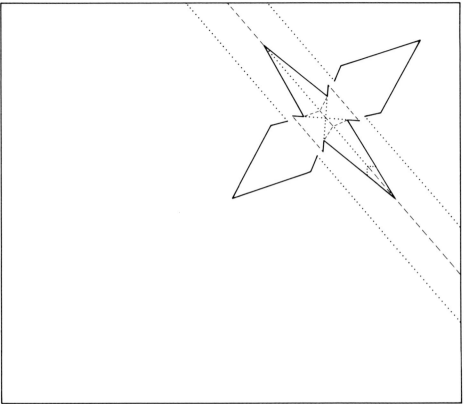

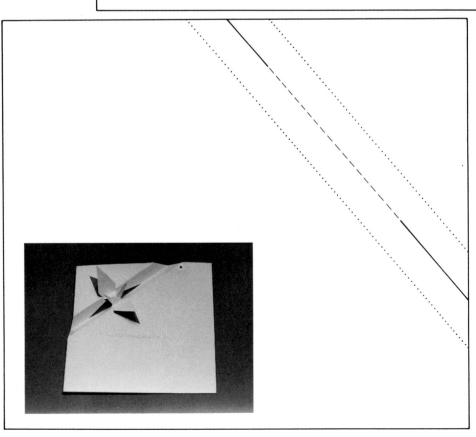

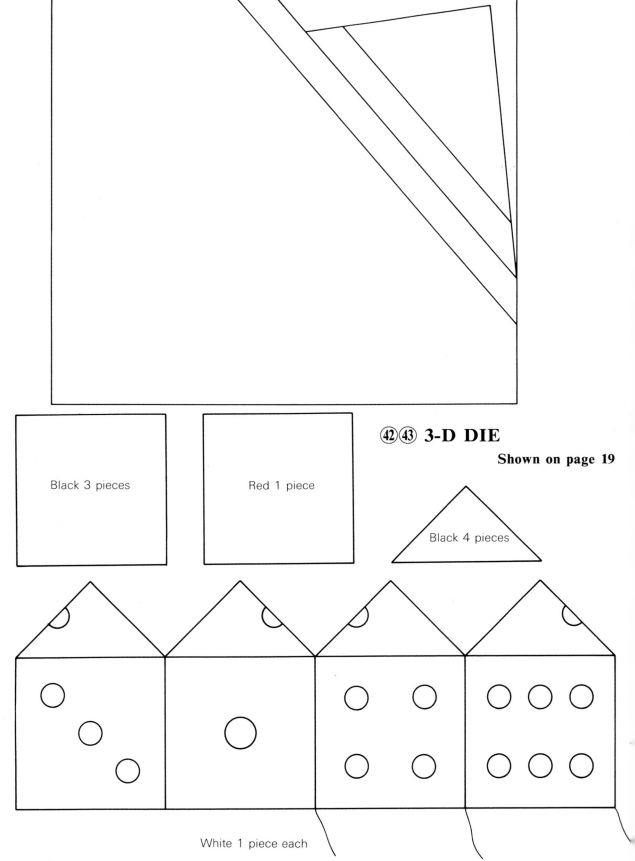

Black 3 pieces

Red 1 piece

**42 43 3-D DIE**

**Shown on page 19**

Black 4 pieces

White 1 piece each

## Materials:
3 Sheets white Bristol paper
15cm × 20cm (6″ × 8″)
1 Sheet glossy red paper
4cm × 4cm (1½″ × 1½″)
4 Sheets glossy black paper
4cm × 4cm (1½″ × 1½″)
Japanese rice paper
Thread

※ Directions are the same for both of these except
for the orientation of the dots.
Try to make cards
with a variety of orientations.

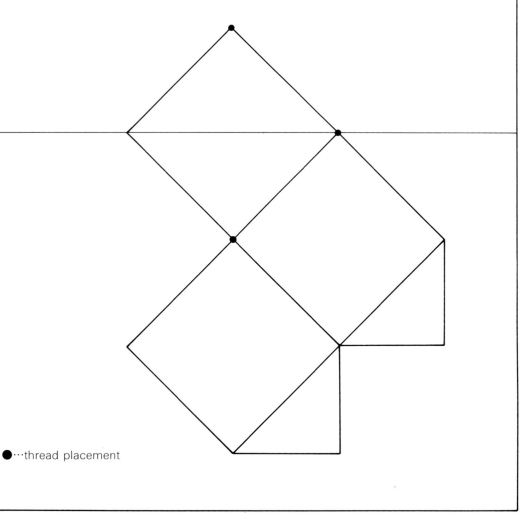

●···thread placement

# ㊺ ALPHABET CARD

**Shown on page 20**

# ㉔ ALPHABET CARD

**Shown on page 20**

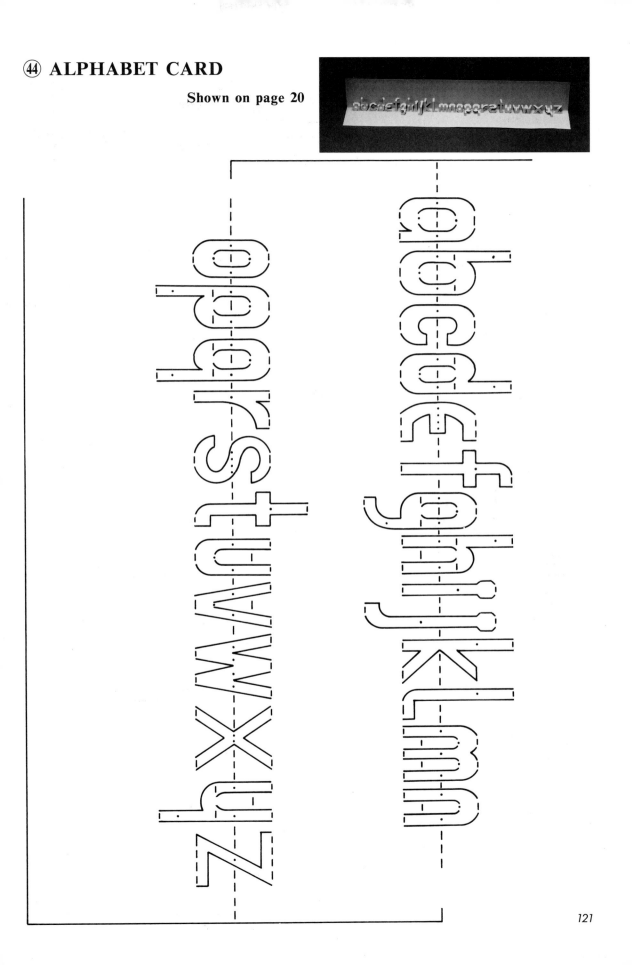

A hobbyist's dream and a great gift, here's an enchanting world of paper pop-ups—the most novel origami books.

### POP-UP ORIGAMIC ARCHITECTURE
*by Masahiro Chatani*

Open the finished cards and—pop!—out come animals, buildings, flowers, or intriguing abstract forms. The possibilities are endless, but author gives readers a solid start with complete instructions for thirty-eight designs. The actual cut-out patterns are given for twenty-four of them, making it easy to begin.

88 pages; 7¼" × 10¼"
A Paperback Original
ISBN 0-87040-656-6

### POP-UP GREETING CARDS
*by Masahiro Chatani*

These delightful pop-up greeting cards—which anyone can have fun making with the simple instructions and ready-made cut-out patterns—were designed by an inventive architect whose handmade cards have been shown at the Museum of Modern Art. They're great for origami hobbyists or anyone who wants to give a truly attention-getting gift or greeting.

96 pages; 7¼" × 10¼"
A Paperback Original
ISBN 0-87040-733-3

### POP-UP PAPER MAGIC
*by Masahiro Chatani*

A memorable business card is literally at your fingertips with this delightful new book of patterns from Masahiro Chatani, the architect who is a genius with cut and folded paper. Seventy different designs, including sports, flowers, birds, animals, and letters of the alphabet. All guaranteed to be memorable!

92 pages; 7¼" × 10¼"
A Paperback Original
ISBN 0-87040-757-0